Correspondence

Correspondence

Models of Letter-Writing from the
Middle Ages to the Nineteenth Century

**Roger Chartier, Alain Boureau
and Cécile Dauphin**

Translated by Christopher Woodall

Princeton University Press
Princeton, New Jersey

Published by Princeton University Press, 41 William Street,
Princeton, New Jersey 08540

Published with the assistance of the French Ministry of Culture

First published in 1997 by Polity Press in association with Blackwell Publishers Ltd.

ISBN 0-691-01696-8

This book has been composed in 11 on 13 pt Sabon

Princeton University Press books are printed on acid-free paper and meet the guidelines for permanence and durability of the Committee on Production Guidelines for Book Longevity of the Council on Library Resources

Printed in Great Britain

1 3 5 7 9 10 8 6 4 2

Contents

Acknowledgements

The publishers would like to thank Dr James Raven of Mansfield College, Oxford, for his assistance in the preparation of this book.

Introduction: An Ordinary Kind of Writing

Model letters and letter-writing in ancien régime France

Roger Chartier

From the sixteenth to the eighteenth century, western societies served a long apprenticeship in the culture of the written word. Mastery of reading and writing was far from evenly distributed and wide gaps persisted between different regions, social groups and the sexes. Yet at least in towns and cities a greater number of tradesmen, shopkeepers, artisans and even journeymen could now read, put their signature to parish registers or notarial deeds, draw up a receipt, keep an accounts book or write a letter. Across the length and breadth of Europe, a specialized literature came into being, whose aim it was to regulate and control ordinary forms of writing, first by explaining and instilling in people the difficult techniques that writing entailed and then by setting out the rules and conventions proper to each written genre.

In the broad array of such didactic texts, *secrétaires* or collections of model letters possessed a special and central place. Theirs was an ancient tradition that dated back to the formularies used in mediaeval chancelleries and they were produced in the vernacular language of every European country.[1] At the outset their intended audience was anything but popular in that they belonged to a genre of books on civility or treatises on social etiquette that targeted a courtly audience or, at the very least, society's elites. Yet in France, *secrétaires* figured prominently in the catalogues of chapbook sellers and later appeared in mainstream publishers' lists. It is therefore reasonable to suppose that they reached the most broad-based and popular of readerships. That is the starting point of this book, sustained by a variety of theoretical perspectives that go far beyond its immediate point of focus.

The first of these perspectives takes the form of a question regarding the usages and meanings that a community of readers, at a given moment in history, assigns to the texts that it appropriates. To be quite sure that they complied with standard rules, popular letter-writers first had to be readers. By way of the insight that *secrétaires* provide, the interrogation of ordinary writing thus brings us to another everyday practice: reading. The relationship that 'popular' readers might entertain with the letter-writing manuals that mainstream publishing made available to them is informed by the tension between text and reading that Michel de Certeau has pinpointed:

> Whether it is a question of newspapers or Proust, the text has a meaning only through its readers; it changes along with them; it is ordered in accordance with codes of perception that it does not control. It becomes a text only in its relation to the exteriority of the reader, by an interplay of implications and ruses between two sorts of 'expectation' in combination: the expectation that organizes a *readable* space (a literality), and one that organizes a procedure necessary for the *actualization* of the work (a reading).[2]

Here, the 'readable space' is that of a particular category of texts – the letter-writing manual collections – and the reading, that of the purchasers of such humble printed matter.

This book embraces a second line of questioning. Letter-writing is one sort of 'ordinary', everyday and private writing, like the accounts book, the recipe book or the family record book.[3] It represents the appropriation and use of a form of competence (the ability to write) outside of those places that regulate its acquisition (an elementary school, a master writer's stall, a charity school), establishing a set of institutionalized practices that restrict its exercise (in front of the priest, notary, judge or administrator). Writing 'without qualities' or without authority therefore seems foreign to the drive to accumulate, totalize and dominate which, in the view of Michel de Certeau, characterizes the 'scriptural economy'. Perhaps paradoxically, it seems closer to the kind of shrewd and tactical writing whose predatory skill it shares: in its own way, it is a kind of 'making do' – and a making do that involves forms of knowhow that have been instilled, rules that have been imposed and models that have been supplied.[4] Close examination of *secrétaires*, their prescriptions, their circulation and their reception thus provides an exemplary indication of both the fundamental tension that articulates strategies of domination, whether physical or symbolic, and the inventiveness of appropriations that governs all the practices of everyday life.

Letter-writing manuals

In the nineteenth century, faltering letter-writers had two possible recourses: either they could take themselves off to the stall of the public writer who, in exchange for ready cash, would take up a pen on their behalf, or they could copy out the formulas and models supplied by letter-writing manuals. Between about 1830 and the turn of the century, this genre enjoyed considerable success: Cécile Dauphin, who has compiled a preliminary inventory, was able to identify 195 titles, published in 616 different editions by 143 different publishers. This mass of scattered material is organized around three chronological landmarks. First of all, the 1850s was the decade when, for the first time, the number of *secrétaires* bearing an author's name exceeded the number of anonymous titles. This signals the end of the tradition of chapbook publishing whereby the genre was generally designated by titles lacking any proper name but covering many and different editions: one need only think of all those editions in the first half of the nineteenth century that were published under the title *Nouveau Secrétaire Français*. Thus endowed with a new identity, the production of *secrétaires* peaked in the years between 1850 and 1869: more than 250 editions appeared during this twenty-year period. There followed a sharp and rapid downturn: the teaching of writing, now understood as the ability to draft texts – including letters – had shifted to the schools. At the very moment when the output of *secrétaires* began to wane, school manuals took to incorporating exemplary letters, supplied as worthy of imitation, and the epistolary form became a regular part of French *dictée* and composition.[5]

Of those authors who put their signatures to letter-writing manuals, most were men. The minority role played by women (accounting for just 20 per cent of named authors) – mainly society women, authors of manuals on *savoir vivre* or of novels – contrasts sharply with the very frequent depiction by the century's painters (Madame Vigée-Lebrun, Devéria and Renoir come to mind) of women readers or letter-writers. Yet this still marks a step forward for women's letter-writing given that in the seventeenth century women accounted for only 2 per cent of published letter collections and in the eighteenth century for only 5 per cent.[6] That authors of letter-writing manuals in the nineteenth century tended overwhelmingly to be men is illustrated (literally) in the books themselves. Engravings depicting the writing of a letter feature a man twenty-seven times and a woman only five times.

The essential question raised by letter-writing manuals is that of their usefulness. There is in fact both direct and indirect evidence on this: the former is to be found in surviving letters where formulas of politesse have been clumsily copied out; the latter consists of disparaging remarks about the practice of resorting to manuals made by letter-writers who sought thus to demonstrate their sincerity or excuse their awkwardness. Yet the impression lingers of a gulf dividing the social world portrayed in the *secrétaires* from that of most apprentice letter-writers. Either aristocratic or bourgeois, organized around formalities and rigid conventions, arranged in hierarchies that accorded with the traditional criteria of dependency and protection, letter-writing manuals appeared remote from the needs or the skills of ordinary readers. Must one conclude that *secrétaires* were not aimed at an ordinary readership at all but at a petty and middling bourgeoisie eager to soak up the ways of the world? Should one suppose that their aim was in fact less practical than their titles and prefaces declared, given that they emphasized ad nauseam that the true art of letter-writing resided not in imitation but in 'naturalness'?

Before attempting to answer these questions, it seemed necessary to take a step back. This has taken the form of an examination of those letter-writing manuals which, during the seventeenth and eighteenth centuries, through the medium of chapbook publishing, reached the most popular of contemporary readers. Even more than in the following century, there appears to be a chasm separating the content of the texts included in the Bibliothèque bleue and the clientele to whom booksellers and chapmen sold these inexpensive books in large quantities. While scorning cultivated genres (such as educational humanist treatises or collections of familiar letters) and professional manuals (such as those drafted by secretaries and master writers or those aimed at merchants), the booksellers and publishers of Troyes, and their emulators too, displayed a paradoxical preference for works which, like those compiled by Puget de La Serre, belonged to the literature of the court. This raises a most basic question: of what possible use can such collections of rules and models have been to the majority of their readers?

There is after all a striking discrepancy between these urbane and lettered *secrétaires* and the audience for the Bibliothèque bleue. It is a discrepancy that is at once chronological and social: chronological, given that the Troyes publishers continued until the last days of the ancien régime to reprint texts first published more than a century and a half earlier; and social, given that the circumstances, subjects, forms and letters presented as models were appropriate to aristocratic society and thoroughly alien to the day-to-day existence of the vast majority of the kingdom's inhabitants. To comprehend the reasons for the 'popular' circulation of works that appear so ill-suited to their declared educational and practical purpose, one has to ponder a number of hypotheses regarding the ways in which they may have been read – ways that would have had nothing to do with any immediately practical function. To read a *secrétaire* might be to learn about the ordering of the social world, strictly translated into the formalities of the letter-writing code; or it might mean penetrating a remote and 'exotic' universe, that of aristocratic ways; or again it might bring with it the pleasure of piecing together a plot from the series of letters furnished as examples for imitation. Model letters were not therefore merely resources provided to people who wanted to write a letter but had not mastered the conventions of letter-writing. More subtly, through a process of readings that were often not followed by any attempt at writing, they nourished a social knowhow and a social imaginary.

This first step back enables us to locate the genre of the letter-writing manual in relation to the meanings that in the seventeenth and eighteenth centuries clung to the term *secrétaire*. For ancien régime language dictionaries, a *secrétaire* was, at one and the same time, an official or clerk, a book, and a piece of furniture (as far as this last acceptation is concerned, at least from the *Dictionnaire de Trévoux*, 1771, onward: 'One also calls *secrétaire* a kind of table or raised bureau in the form of a school desk, in which there are several drawers that can be locked by key, where one can shut away important papers'). Letter-writing is thus perceived as a practice that is the reserve of professionals; as a special competence that can be acquired through the instruction of masters; and as an individual act, performed in privacy. In these links between correspondence and secrecy, etymology asserts its full rights since *secretum* designates, at once, a place of retirement, secret thoughts or words, and secret papers.

Mastery of the secrets of the art of writing has always been the object of competition. By retracing the mediaeval invention of the letter-writing norm, Alain Boureau has focused attention on the original contention and rivalry that dispossessed the writing masters, the *dictatores*, of the monopoly that they had established over the rhetoric of the letter and that secured the triumph of the notaries and jurists. Epistolary convention is, in a twofold way, heir to these origins. On the one hand, *ars dictaminis* for a long time ensured that the letter belonged to the genre of eloquence. A strong and durable link was thus wrought between correspondence and the spoken word, whether this took the form of the dictation of a letter to a scribe or that of the reading aloud, for all those present, of the missive just received. On the other hand, mediaeval epistolary rhetoric refined the subtle balances that guaranteed that the style and form of the letter (in particular superscriptions and subscriptions) were proportional to the gap in condition separating the letter-writer and the addressee. Ancien régime *secrétaires* and, subsequently, nineteenth-century manuals scrupulously respected these devices which essentially served to define the civility of correspondence.

Two fundamental lessons can be drawn from the study of model letters. The first emphasizes the need always to postulate a possible gap between, on the one hand, the intentions that prompt the writing, publication and circulation of texts and, on the other hand, the ways that they may then be used and read. The educational purpose which quite evidently underpinned the large-scale spread of model letters in no way implies that all their purchasers, or even a majority of them, became letter-writers who complied with the conventions they had been taught, or even that they ever wrote a single letter. The huge gulf separating the initial purpose of the texts and the skills and needs of their 'popular' readers necessarily raises the hypothesis of unforeseen kinds of readings, quite detached from any practical usefulness, thus catapulting educational exemplars into the register of fiction. The *secrétaires* included in the Bibliothèque bleue provide a nice example of the creative and silent detours that characterize reading, while also testifying to the inventiveness of consumers who are never either totally constrained or totally overwhelmed by the symbolic wares furnished for their consumption.

But – and this is the second lesson – those who are in a position to dominate writing always conceive of it as something capable of imposing discipline on everyday life. The tight and rigorous rules entailed in learning to write constitute one of the severest constraints that can be exercised on bodies of experts.[7] The monopoly of legitimacy, so hotly disputed by professionals of the written word (master writers, school-teachers, notaries, clerks and public writers) is a mark of the powers that the ability to write could confer, in a society still only partially literate, on those who exercised it either on their own or on others' behalf.[8] Finally, by announcing the prescriptions to be observed and the examples to be imitated, manuals on writing fulfilled a dual function: they established strict control over the production of written matter – even in its ordinary forms; and they distinguished between the learned, who complied naturally with the conventions that civility required, and the uncouth, whose use of writing was as yet untamed. Model letter collections were thus trapped in an insoluble contradiction: they furnished for imitation by the unskilful (or less skilful) a set of rules and examples whose professional and social value resided precisely in the fact that they had been confiscated by a body of specialists or by a particular milieu. Devoted to disseminating a form of knowhow whose value depended on its exclusivity, the status of ancien régime *secrétaires* was inevitably ambiguous and unstable, like that of a secret that was bruited abroad.

The 1847 postal enquiry

This retrospective study of model letters grew out of research into letter-writing in nineteenth-century France.[9] The starting point for this collective investigation was the examination of a truly exceptional document, a set of 343 volumes kept with the Bibliothèque Nationale's collection of French manuscripts and entitled *Relevé par département du nombre de communes et autres localités ayant une appellation propre en France, d'après le résultat de l'enquête générale faite au mois de novembre 1847 par les soins de l'Administration des Postes.*[10] By this date, every post office manager had received forms and a circular requesting him to furnish a variety of information relating to each commune located within his postal area, entering the said information under four headings: the 'movement of correspondence observed over two weeks', 'statistical information' (on the population, surface area and types of employment within the commune as well as its distance from the post office), the 'situation of the letter box' on the territory of the commune, and a 'nomenclature of hamlets, castles, factories, farms, isolated houses and whatsoever inhabited places having a particular name, dependent on the commune'. The first chart in the questionnaire, giving a commune by commune breakdown of all correspondence dispatched and received between 14 and 28 November 1847, is a gift to any historian eager to put some numbers on the volume and geography of epistolary exchange in nineteenth-century France.

Given that the investigation was at the behest of the Directeur Général des Postes, the statistics had to be precise. They were structured in accordance with three main sets of distinctions. First, that between letters sent to addresses within the commune and those collected there, whether 'taken from the rural box', or 'collected by hand during the course of the rural postman's round'. Second, that between letters circulating within the post office's own postal area (roughly equivalent to that of a canton or district) and those that either came from corresponding offices or were dispatched thither: letters within one's own postal area being taxed at 10 centimes, those sent further afield according to the distance covered. The third was between different postal objects: letters, newspapers and printed matter, and letters and parcels addressed to state employees which circulated duty-free. Evidence relating to 32,459 communes was collected for the 1847 postal enquiry, providing an enormous mass of data, unique for the nineteenth century.

One's enthusiasm should, however, be moderated. France had not been surveyed in its entirety, far from it. The communes covered by the survey, while they made up 88 per cent of the total number, were home to only 67 per cent of the French population. Furthermore, the correspondence received by these communes accounted for only 35 per cent of the total mass of post circulating within France, and that dispatched by the communes surveyed accounted for only 17 per cent of the total. The France surveyed by the 1847 postal enquiry was above all a France of rural areas, of communes comprising fewer than 2,000 inhabitants, a country much less given to letter-writing than the France of the cities and small towns that did not complete – indeed, had not been asked to complete – the forms issued by the Direction Générale des Postes.

Yet for all its wealth of information and all its limitations, the 1847 postal enquiry has held the interest of historians. Mostly it has been used as a basis for monographs, centring on a particular region[11] or on a specific postal object (such as the newspaper). In 1975, however, on the initiative of Jacques Ozouf and as part of an enquiry that he and François Furet were conducting into the spread of literacy among the French,[12] the enquiry evidence was at last examined systematically. Hitherto unused, this huge set of data was computerized and became the main source for our investigation into the uses of letter-writing.

The first question raised by the 1847 postal enquiry is: why was it undertaken? In 1849, a poster appeared in every post office informing the French people of a major reform:

> The public is hereby notified that as from the first of January 1849 the tax on letters hitherto calculated according to the distance covered has been abolished and replaced by a fixed and uniform tax

> of 20 centimes for any letter circulating within the country provided its weight does not exceed 7 grams and a half and regardless of the distance to be covered throughout France, Corsica and Algeria.

A new mode of postage was thus made possible, since the sender could now use stamps or postmarks to the value of the postal tax. If the old method of payment (by the addressee on receiving the post) survived, what disappeared was the principle that postage would be levied in proportion to the distance separating the place from which the letter was dispatched and the place to which it was addressed.

Another question is whether or not the postal enquiry of 1847 was in some way linked to the debates that ushered in the postal reform. It would appear not. Its purpose was quite different. Above all, it aimed to compile a postal service dictionary listing all the places where people dwelt and which had to be visited by rural postmen 'at least one day out of two'. The postman's round, introduced in 1830, had broken with the previous arrangement which obliged the addressee – who was notified 'by all the occasions that might offer themselves', as a circular published in 1808 expressed it – to go and pick up the post from the post office. Once post had to be delivered, it was essential to draw up a list of the communes, hamlets and out of the way places that had to be provided with the service. Already twelve years old, the 1835 *Dictionnaire des Postes* needed revising and extending. Hence the need for an enquiry and hence too its shortcomings. Since the main goal was to carry out a census of inhabited places scattered across country communes, neither cities nor main offices had to be covered by the enquiry forms. The mass of material gathered through the zeal of the post office heads was put to little practical administrative use: the 1859 *Dictionnaire des Postes* listed only three inhabited places per commune, and the part of the enquiry that set out to measure the ebb and flow of post was never subjected to overall statistical scrutiny.

The investigation conducted by Cécile Dauphin, Pierrette Lebrun-Pezerat and Danièle Poublan was the first to make full use of a document that had been overlooked by those who commissioned it.[13] The mass of evidence thus made available traces a clear map of the space occupied by letter-writing prior to the transformation of the French social fabric. The gap that existed in the rural France covered by the postal enquiry between the number of letters received (6.3 per 100 inhabitants over the 15 days in question) and the number of letters sent (2.8) underscores the role of towns and cities as the main centres from which correspondence was dispatched. The gap that separates the number of letters leaving the postal area (7.2 letters per 100 inhabitants over the 15 days) and the number that were dispatched to addresses within the same postal area (1.9) highlights the rarity of recourse to communication by letter in the immediate vicinity – where people still preferred to make contact by means of a short journey or by word of mouth. However, for distances of over 100 kilometres or so, letter writing and sending just dried up. The cost of postage was prohibitive with a system where it increased with distance.

As the maps testify, mid nineteenth-century France was not uniform in its use of letter-writing. At first sight, the picture that emerges is unsurprising: letter-writing France covers by and large the same ground as the educated, wealthy and healthy France that the political arithmeticians of the Restoration habitually placed to the north of an imaginary line bisecting the nation from Saint-Malo to Geneva.[14] Yet in reality things were much less straightforward, with marked peaks and troughs appearing *within* each of these two areas. To the north of the Saint-Malo–Geneva line, a 'lettered' heart, comprising the Île-de-France, Champagne, Burgundy and the Orléanais, stood out from more peripheral areas where people read and wrote fewer letters. To the south, the area around Lyons and the Mediterranean coastal strip made a far better showing than the epistolary wastelands of Brittany, the Massif Central or the Pyrenees.

What reasons were there for this geography of contrasts? The explanations that spring immediately to mind are not necessarily the best ones. Given that the correlation between literacy and letter-writing is generally strong, the numerous mismatches make it necessary to draw a clear distinction between what it means to learn to write at school, a mere matter of mastering script, and the ability to produce texts (hence letters) that is possessed by only some of the literate. The sense of despair expressed in the life stories of certain clumsy letter-writers, who none the less knew how to read and write, gives an indication of a gulf that left many of those who had learnt to read and write feeling powerless and miserable when it came to complying with the regulations and conventions of letter writing. If, in the nineteenth century, people continued to delegate the task of writing, it was not only because literacy became universal rather late in the day. It was also because those who knew how to write but who could not compose a letter had no choice but to rely on the skills of someone else (the mayor or the schoolmaster, the child who attended school or the more literate friend).

Competence after all does not necessarily entail practice, any more than the existence of an infrastructure entails its use. This is demonstrated by the gaps between the postal network as formed by the location of post offices and the practice of writing and sending letters. A heavy concentration of post offices did not always translate into high rates of letter posting. Other factors have to be borne in mind if one is to understand the postal geography of mid nineteenth-century France. First, there was administrative work that gave county towns their epistolary lead: an average of 11.5 letters received and 10.8 letters dispatched per 100 inhabitants over the 15 days. Yet it is worth noting that although communes of this type all had exactly the same functions to fulfil, there were marked differences between different regions, as if county towns displayed a kind of overriding solidarity with the geographical areas to which they belonged. Moreover, pattern of settlement was a more decisive factor than population size: even small communes with a grouped settlement pattern boasted higher rates of epistolary activity than more populous communes that had a scattered settlement pattern. Lastly, it is economic development that seems most powerfully to have determined rates of letter-writing and the variations between them. There is indeed a very strong correlation (0.84) between postal activity and aggregate economic indicators.[15]

This conclusion completely overturns received perceptions by situating a practice that has been traditionally associated with intimate communication and the expression of feelings within the context of business turnover, commercial ebbs and flows and manufacturing industry. In its bald measurements and painstaking correlations, the statistical and cartographic treatment of the 1847 enquiry has supported the estimates of contemporaries who judged that eight or nine letters out of every ten were business letters. This useful reminder should go some way to correcting any hasty perception that might link letter-writing to the realm of family, friendship and love.

The letter depicted

When records make this possible, letter-writing manuals can therefore be contrasted with the practices they were supposed to govern. Similarly, they should be contrasted with surviving depictions of letter-writing.

Between 26 July 1837 and 6 February 1839, the cartoonist Gavarni published thirty-three prints, under the collective title *La boîte aux lettres*, in the satirical paper *Le Charivari* which Maison Aubert began publishing in 1832 under the editorship of Charles Philipon. This series (completed by a thirty-fourth print which never appeared in *Le Charivari*) provides a wonderful glimpse of the values and functions that at that time were so spontaneously attached to letter-writing that they were open to mockery and caricature. Comparison between these images, which were printed less than a decade before the postal enquiry, and life stories or 'popular' autobiographies[16] serves to indicate to what extent the new letter-writers shared the clichés and received ideas that, at the start of the nineteenth century and no doubt earlier, were associated with correspondence.

The environment of ordinary people was not overlooked by Gavarni's series. The world of female domesticity was illustrated by the young maid reading a letter addressed to her mistress, by the cook in her kitchen writing to her lover whom she fears is inconstant, and by the two young serving women who have broken the bounds of their condition: one has put aside the housework to sit herself down at the desk of her master and mistress and write to the man she loves; the other declares to her boyfriend in the letter that she is about to slip into the postbox, 'I am proud of my outfit my mistress is to the country and I've tried a dress a hat a mantilla of hers, all of it suits me superbly.' Beneath each image Gavarni engraved a caption whose script and spelling complemented the caricature of the supposed letter-writer. The world of the workshop and small shop was represented by a craftsman writing to the minister of finance to inform him that he could not pay his tax.

Like craftsmen and workmen autobiographers, these men and women of the people had acquired the self-assurance that enabled them, whatever the difficulties, to write a letter. Two of them, however, still had to rely on someone else's skills. A young girl is portrayed using the services of an elderly letter-writer, whose eyesight is poor and hand unsteady – as one can tell from the messy crossing-out in the love letter that he is drafting. A woman milliner dictates a letter intended for her lover to one of her friends, who uses the lid of a hat box resting on her lap as a writing surface. Here we have an illustration of two forms of delegated letter-writing: the first, more traditional, dating back to the ancien régime, features a paid professional, the letter-writer; the second and more recent scene, depicting a situation encountered in life stories, rests on the cultural difference that within one and the same family and within one and the same social environment marked out those men and women who knew how to write a letter from those men and women who did not.[17]

In Gavarni's prints, the main comic spring lies in subverting the taken-for-granted link between letter-writing and secrecy. This process can take two forms. A letter may be read by someone to whom it was not addressed. For example, there is the husband, a huntsman, who stumbles upon the letter his wife has sent to her lover ('dearest, *he* is going hunting tomorrow come at nine o'clock to the garden'); or the servant who, without breaking the seal, manages to read her mistress's missive ('there is now between us, oh my beloved, a mystery that no human sight must penetrate'); or, again, owing to the indelicacy of the letter's addressee, the occasion when three friends, fine gentlemen all, set about reading together the letter that one of them has received and that runs, 'You possess the secret of my life . . . oh my beloved Alfred, you shan't betray it, shall you?' Alternatively, a letter may be delivered or posted or read to or in front of the very person whom it is intended to dupe: thus, it is while taking a walk on her husband's arm that a woman casts into the box a letter in which she grants her lover a rendez-vous; thus, it is the young mistress of a 'man of letters' who brings him the invitation to an evening of debauchery;

thus, it is before the very bearer of a letter of recommendation that its addressee reads the text which advises him to get rid of the intruder. This last image recalls the practice current in Renaissance Italy of placing a discreet and secret mark on those letters of recommendation that were intended to be taken seriously.

Secrecy, whether betrayed or closely guarded, was automatically assumed to be the letter's main attribute. And it was the bounds of this secrecy that laws regarding correspondence had to define: on the death of their addressee ought personal letters to be restored to their senders? Did husbands have the right to open letters received by their wives? These were questions that by the end of the century were engaging both the legal profession and journalists in heated debate. Yet ordinary letter-writers did not seem to place such a high value on the confidentiality of the letter. The drafting of letters often involved two or more people, they were often aimed at different addressees in succession and they were often read out aloud: these are the features that were generally associated with correspondence in accounts given in the life stories of workers, craftsmen and peasants. For them, epistolary practice did not demand the kind of secrecy that ideally should protect confidences exchanged between two intimate correspondents. Quite the reverse: at the level of the community – whether family, village, workmates or political associates, etc. – the goal of letter-writing was to cement, maintain and extend the bonds of social life and solidarity. Whatever secrets there were had nothing to do with any individual consciousness but rather formed the basis of the specific identity of a whole group, constructed by the process of exchange between those who belonged to it.

In these popular representations, it is felt that letters have no choice but to state the truth of an experience, the force of a will, the seriousness of an undertaking. Acquired with a struggle, competence at letter-writing was not to be prostituted: it delivered what was most essential in existence. But for the letter-writers that Gavarni caricatured, things were different. For them, letters were lies: having just risen from his mistress's bed, a student writes to his uncle asking him for money ('I'm working night and day but I'm very short of money; books are that expensive in Paris'); a young girl, in her dressing gown and with her hair falling loose, informs a sergeant-major that the corporal, her lover, who behind her is having his hair done, will not be able to return to barracks because he is ill; or, again, two young women compare the letters they have received from one and the same man, both proclaiming his ardent passion. When letters are sincere and touching, they are betrayed by the way they are read. It is while playing cards, with two bottles of wine by his side, that a man reads, without a trace of emotion, the following sad lines: 'Oh! pity the cruel state in which my attachment for you leaves me!' And the fine and sentimental letter that Ernest has received from his lover ('I have your letter, darling, I press it to my heart and cover it with my kisses. How sweet it is for me to think that you are doing the same with mine') is turned by another of his lovers into curlpapers which can then be used to curl the hair of this doubly beloved young man.

To contrast these two sets of representations – Gavarni's prints and the descriptions given in the 'popular' life stories – is not to set two realities against one other, the one bourgeois, the other that of craftsmen, workers or peasants. The attitudes of one social grouping or the other might just as well be inverted. In bourgeois families, correspondence could also be a collective practice weaving a social network and cementing the exchange of goods, information and services. Likewise, certain 'popular' letter-writers put their most secret of thoughts and emotions into the letters they wrote. The stereotypes point to something rather different: two distinct ways of relating to the written word. For those who had, as it were, inherited the ability to write, literacy was shorn of its gravity and could be manipulated with ease. For others who had paid for their mastery with a perhaps painful break from their former background, the written word brought with it great expectations: the chance of emancipation, the creation of memory and the fraternity of bonds that could be preserved despite absence.

Business affairs, the family and sharing secrets

The statistics, however, are clear: the correlation that best accounts for the use of letter-writing in mid nineteenth-century France is that between postal activity and economic development.

At the time of the 1847 enquiry, postal geography and business geography went hand in hand. In those cases where surviving collections of letters were assembled in ways which make it possible to consider them as representative of the general run of letters posted, they support the conclusion drawn from the statistical evidence. This is the case, for example, with the 608 letters dispatched from Paris between 1830 and 1865 and kept in the collection of postmarks at the Musée de la Poste in Paris. The reason why these letters were kept has nothing whatever to do with the nature of the texts in question since the only aim here was to collect the marks stamped on them by the postal workers. It is precisely because this sample is so random, assigning no priority to any particular category of letter, that it is of general value.[18]

Analysis of this corpus confirms contemporary perceptions inasmuch as it underlines the preponderant place occupied by business letters of one kind or another. Indeed, commercial and banking letters account for 47 per cent of the total, while letters sent by notaries, advocates, solicitors and bailiffs account for 38 per cent. Only 12 per cent of the corpus (15 per cent if one includes announcements of weddings, births, deaths, etc.) are of a personal, private or intimate nature, which roughly accords with contemporary estimates that put them at a tenth of all post sent. The process of counting and reading these letters casts doubt on several classical images. The automatic association of letters with intimate outpourings and the view that correspondence is a relation between two individuals are both called into question. Indeed, like those letters portrayed in popular life stories, many of the Musée de la Poste letters are addressed to several people at once and were clearly intended to be read aloud before an entire gathered household. Another classical image, inspired by pictorial representations of women writing (or reading) letters, made the woman the correspondent *par excellence*: in the sample, however, only 5 per cent of the letters are addressed to a woman and only 2 per cent are written by one.

Any typology of nineteenth-century post should however beware of making sharp distinctions. Business and the expression of feeling could go together. Commercial letters often made room for family news or chitchat. Conversely, letters exchanged between members of the same family served above all to gather information (about advantageous matches or about servants or craftspeople worthy of employment), to make requests for goods or services, to recover outstanding debts from stubborn creditors, or to administer properties jointly owned. Printed communications, which became more common during the course of the century, reveal the same ambiguities. While some adhered firmly to the 'business' register (prospectuses, circulars, summonses and administrative papers, etc.), others, like wedding announcements or visiting cards, further swelled the more or less extended network of family or social relations. Besides, handwriting found its way on to these new objects, invading their margins, headings and spaces, to the point where the postal administration became concerned and decided in 1859 to impose tax on any such strange and handwritten additions.

There is therefore no clear opposition between the general run of letters and the collections of family correspondence that have formed the subject of numerous studies over the last few years.[19] What such studies have demonstrated above all is that family correspondences are always the result of a process of construction that entails sorting, scrapping and keeping. The very existence and make-up of a family correspondence represents a record of the series of actions which, over generations, have conserved one portion of all the letters written and received as fit witnesses to the family identity. Though chance may at times affect what disappears and what is kept, its role should not be overstated. After all, not all letters have the same chance of survival. The prospects for a letter's survival are best when its addressee has assumed the task of spokesperson or record keeper for the family memory, when it has been sent by close relatives and when the family has not changed residence for many decades. Passed on and handed down, gathered together and placed in an order, correspondences that have been sent or received by the members of a single family (and, most frequently, exchanged between them) acquire a new status, a new function – that of ensuring the continuity and stability of the line. If letters, taken separately, can be related to the single moments when they were written or sent, their gathering together into a single archive has another meaning: that denoted by the act of collecting.

Every letter, by describing where and when it is being written and by mentioning other letters (received, expected or hoped for), takes as its main topic the pact that binds the correspondents. The real subject matter of letter-writing is the writing of the letters. In their efforts to represent this process, however, women and men do not bring the same motifs into play. Women, who often write on behalf of the whole family, describe a practice that does not have its own special site within the home and which is always interrupted by the presence of others (especially children), a practice which recalls the duty of letter-writing as it was inculcated during their childhood when as little girls they would write under the watchful eye of their mother. Men, on the other hand, steal from business hours any moments they devote to family correspondence, emphasizing the solitary nature of writing, whether in their office or on their travels. Both men and women, in the bourgeois or aristocratic world which is generally that of family correspondence, are familiar with the rules and conventions that must preside over the composition of every letter. But they also know that epistolary art entails no slavish imitation of scrupulously observed models, but ease and naturalness. They are able to play freely upon the detailed codes set out in the *secrétaires* because they have interiorized them well enough to be able to turn them on their heads. Yet their freedom to write what they think fit is not without its limitations. It remains subject to what is authorized by the degree of proximity in kinship, age and condition between writer and addressee.

Over the long run, family correspondences create a sediment, a basis for memory. At the time they are written, they form a network that places the particular existence of each individual and his or her closest relations within the solidarities of a 'kinship front'. The exchange of letters criss-crossing between family members is a prime means of safeguarding links that distance places in jeopardy. The regular and obligatory letter demonstrates to everyone on each occasion the existence of a community that is constantly given form in the request for services, the reciprocal errands, whether of a material or sentimental kind, and the fulfilment itself, whether emphasized or solicited, of the undertaking to exchange letters. Family letters, sometimes the work of several hands and even more often read aloud by several people, often passed on or copied out, were not the place for intimate outpourings. They demanded restraint and a strict self-censorship that could only be lifted when the person writing could count on the discretion of his or her addressee.

If the temptation to share confidences, like the temptation to make more intimate confessions of a kind permitted by a bond of spiritual affinity between two people, often makes an appearance in these family letters, a strong sense of reserve persists. It is as if letter-writers, caught between the demands of the family network and their desire for a closer rapport, had no choice but to eschew the more direct expressions of feeling. This is not to say that emotions, desires and passions were absent from these letters. Prudishly couched in euphemistic terms, masked by the conventions of a timid epistolary language and strong social demands, emotions always hovered just beneath the surface. Family correspondence did not suffocate the temptation towards intimacy: it bound it into its own forms and obligations.

Model letters and collections of correspondences in their different ways bear the hallmarks of some of the main developments that transformed French society between the Middle Ages and the nineteenth century. The forward march of literacy, spreading the skill that was essential if writing was no longer to be delegated to someone else – a local worthy, a professional letter-writer or a relative – was the first of these long-term shifts. But the circumstances in which people gained access to writing – like its geography – did not necessarily match the circumstances and geography of letter-writing: the acquisition of a skill did not by itself ensure that the skill would be put to practical use. For that to happen, other triggers were necessary.

The construction of an administrative and bureaucratic state, the opening up of the economy and increased geographical mobility were the most powerful of these factors.[20] By opening up geographical areas that in many cases had long remained isolated and by forcing people to establish relations over greater distances, these different (and frequently uneven) processes multiplied the circumstances under which it was necessary to write a letter. This is clearly borne out by the increasing and often overwhelming proportion of letters concerning matters of business (commerce, banking, law, administration, etc.) featured in collections of epistolary models, in surviving letter collections (provided the reason they survived was random in nature), and also in the overall volumes of correspondence flows.

It is upon this fundamental link between 'business' and letter-sending that a further long-term shift – the emergence of a sphere of individuality and privacy – may be seen to hinge. The exchange of letters reveals two variants of this, which are often overlaid. The first, a social variant, sees the destiny of the individual, the couple or the family unit as wholly dependent on the maintenance of a strong network of kinship. Correspondence between the members of a family (broadly defined) is seen as a particularly effective means of expressing and reinforcing the 'family front' which sustains that state of reciprocal (and beneficial) dependency that unites the individual family members. But while circulating useful information, goods and services, this form of letter-writing practice is not the right place for confiding one's secrets. Confidences belong in the second variant of the private sphere, consisting of elective affinities between bosom friends. Here, the job of correspondence is no longer to maintain the cohesion of one's kin; it becomes instead, even when addressed to a close friend or relation, a refuge from the obligations and proprieties of the family.[21] For a time, the conventions and guidelines of *secrétaires* are forgotten, so that passion, sorrow or fantasy may be given an individual and subjective voice.

Secrecy versus the family network, spontaneity versus guidelines: these were the main tensions structuring the practice of letter-writing in ancient societies – those prior to the invention of the telephone.[22] And it is these tensions that we have sought to tease out over the long span of time occupied by model letter collections. The inertia of this genre, the stability of its conventions and the frequency with which old materials were reused obliged us to compare nineteenth-century manuals with those circulating in the seventeenth and eighteenth centuries, at a time when the publishers of popular books were printing aristocratic *secrétaires* that seemed very ill-suited to the needs and skills of the very humble letter-writers who made up their clientele. Venturing still further into the past, we have to tie the letter-writing norm firmly to two references that govern it in the western world: the rhetorical reference provided by the *ars dictaminis* or *ars dictandi* treatises that in the eleventh and twelfth centuries founded a norm, a technique and a skill that promised to have a great future, and a biblical reference, with the central place that the New Testament epistles occupied in the liturgy.

Notes

1 For an inventory of *secrétaires* produced in England, see K. Gee Hornbeak, 'The Complete Letter Writer in England 1586–1800', *Smith College Studies in Modern Languages* 15, nos 3–4 (Apr.–July 1934), pp. 1–150.

2 Michel de Certeau, *The Practice of Everyday Life* (Berkeley: University of California Press, 1984), pp. 170–1.

3 Daniel Fabre (ed.), *Écritures ordinaires* (Paris: P.O.L., 1993).

4 On the possible ways of understanding the writing/reading coupling suggested by the work of Michel de Certeau, see Anne-Marie Chartier and Jean Hébrard, 'L'invention du quotidien, une lecture, des usages', *Le Débat*, no. 49 (Mar.–Apr. 1988), pp. 97–108.

5 Anne-Marie Chartier and Jean Hébrard, 'Lire pour écrire à l'école primaire? L'invention de la composition française dans l'école du XIXe siècle', in Yves Reuteur (ed.), *Les interactions lecture-écriture*, Actes du Colloque Théodile-Crel, Lille, Nov. 1993 (Berne: Peter Lang, 1994), pp. 23–90.

6 Fritz Nies, 'Un genre féminin?', *Revue d'Histoire Littéraire de la France* (1978), no. 6: 'La lettre au XVIIe siècle', pp. 994–1003.

7 Jonathan Goldberg, *Writing Matter: From the Hands of the English Renaissance* (Stanford: Stanford University Press, 1990).

8 Armando Petrucci, 'Per una strategia della mediazione grafica nel Cinquecento italiano', *Archivio Storico Italiano*, 1 (1986), pp. 97–112, and 'Scrivere per gli altri', *Scrittura e Civiltà*, 13 (1989), pp. 475–87.

9 Roger Chartier (ed.), *La Correspondance. Les usages de la lettre au XIXe siècle* (Paris: Fayard, 1991). The first chapter of this book is an extensive account of the 1847 postal enquiry (see n. 13 below).

10 Bibliothèque Nationale, Paris, Ms. fr. 9787–10129.

11 Alain Corbin, *Archaïsme et modernité en Limousin au XIXe siècle, 1845–1889* (Paris: Éditions Marcel Rivière, 1975), pp. 147–51.

12 François Furet and Jacques Ozouf, *Reading and Writing: Literacy in France from Calvin to Jules Ferry* (Cambridge: Cambridge University Press, 1982).

13 Cécile Dauphin, Pierrette Lebrun-Pezerat and Danièle Poublan, with the collaboration of Michel Demonet, 'L'enquête postale de 1847', in Chartier, *La Correspondance*, pp. 21–119.

14 Roger Chartier, 'La ligne Saint-Malo–Genève', in Pierre Nora (ed.), *Les lieux de mémoire*, vol. 3: *Les Frances*, 1: 'Conflits et partages' (Paris: Gallimard, 1992), pp. 739–75.

15 Bernard Lepetit, 'Sur les dénivellations de l'espace économique en France dans les années 1830', *Annales E.S.C.* (1986), pp. 1243–72.

16 Jean Hébrard, 'La lettre représentée. Les pratiques épistolaires populaires dans les récits de vie ouvriers et paysans', in Chartier, *La Correspondance*, pp. 279–365.

17 Armando Petrucci, 'Scrivere per gli altri', and Christine Métatayer, 'Écrivains publics et milieux populaires à Paris sous l'ancien régime. Le cas des écrivains des charniers du cimetière des Saints-Innocents', doctoral thesis, Université Laval, Quebec, 1991.

18 Danièle Poublan, 'Affaires et passions. Des lettres parisiennes au milieu du XIXe siècle', in Chartier, *La Correspondance*, pp. 373–406.

19 See, for example, Caroline Chotard-Lioret, 'Correspondre en 1900, le plus public des actes privés, ou la manière de gérer un réseau de parenté', *Ethnologie Française* (1985), no. 1, pp. 63–71; Marie-Claire Grassi, *L'Art de la lettre au temps de la Nouvelle Héloïse et du romantisme* (Geneva: Éditions Slatkine, 1994), and Cécile Dauphin, Pierrette Lebrun-Pezerat and Danièle Poublan, *Ces bonnes lettres. Une correspondance familiale au XIXe siècle* (Paris: Albin Michel, 1995).

20 Daniele Marchesini, *Il bisogno di scrivere. Usi della scrittura nell'Italia Moderna* (Rome-Bari: Editori Laterza, 1992).

21 Anne Martin-Fugier, 'Les lettres célibataires', in Chartier, *La Correspondance*, pp. 407–26.

22 Philippe Ariès and Georges Duby (eds), *Histoire de la vie privée*, vol. 4: *De la Révolution à la Grande Guerre*, vol. ed. Michelle Perrot (Paris: Éditions du Seuil, 1987). In particular see the contributions from Alain Corbin, Anne Martin-Fugier and Michelle Perrot.

1

The Letter-Writing Norm, a Mediaeval Invention

Alain Boureau

Liveliness in letter-writing lingers and recurs despite the dead hand of petty rules and the slow pace of change. If one compares the 'Epistolary encyclopaedia' (*Summa dictaminis*), written in about 1190 by Bernard of Meung,[1] with any how-to manual on letter-writing currently on sale in our larger shops, certain astonishing continuities are apparent. A few general recommendations quickly make way for a sizable batch of model letters – 501 of them in Bernard of Meung's collection – composed for use in specific situations, seldom or never to recur in the life of the person consulting the manual. The novice letter-writer, confronted with such a hefty manual, at once reassuring and intimidating, becomes aware of the existence of a standard that governs correspondence, one of a set of cultural rules that very clearly lays bare the mechanisms of social reproduction. Not long before Bernard of Meung compiled his collection, Saint Bernard himself penned a very considerable epistolary oeuvre – 500 letters survive, probably half of all those written – without complying with any of the prescriptions of letter-writing technique. Indeed, the very hallmark of distinguished letter-writing is the open contempt that is displayed for rules that are taught but that nobody wants to or can apply.

Correspondence provides a clear sociocultural perspective, bottom-up or top-down, according to one's point of view. Letter-writing creates an illusion of unbounded communication: the humblest citizen may dispatch a missive to the highest reaches of the political, social or cultural hierarchy. Open letters aim to bypass all intermediaries standing between ordinary public opinion and decision-makers. Yet, at the same time, correspondence demonstrates the inaccessible character of true flair: connoisseurs well versed in the works of distinguished authors frequently draw attention to their correspondence as evidence of inimitable and exquisite expressive powers soaring beyond the confines of genre and hard work. The only hope left to the ignorant and the middlebrow is to chase after the scraps of such brilliance in the letter-writing manuals, where the lexical duality of 'art' is made manifest, at once technical skill and creative act.

Historians have the good fortune to be able to observe the birth of this apparently timeless sociocultural mechanism. The first manuals on letter-writing technique made a sudden appearance towards the end of the eleventh century and by the twelfth century already comprised sets of model letters that were both exhaustive and coherent. The Middle Ages invented three forms of rhetoric unknown to the Ancients: sermonizing technique, poetic art and epistolary science. Yet it is this last invention that was to remain the most mysterious: if sermons came into existence with Christianity (at least in the Graeco-Latin world), if versifying technique became necessary with the phonological transformations overtaking the Latin language – which by the first century AD was beginning to lose the prosodic features that had previously structured its poetry – and with the emergence of the various vernaculars, the universal and timeless practice of letter-writing did not seem to demand a new form of rhetoric.

In this chapter my aim is to analyse the mediaeval genealogy of the notion of a letter-writing norm, without attempting an overview of the art of letter-writing in the Middle Ages, a task that has been very well performed by two eminent American mediaevalists, James Murphy and Giles Constable, who recently produced a survey of the abundant and erudite literature now available.[2] My purpose will be not only to explain the emergence of a cultural technique but also to examine how the need to write letters and to comply with appropriate rules was interiorized.

To grasp the significance of the development of a letter-writing norm in the Middle Ages, I shall superimpose two different types of chronology and of historical explanation, which correspond to two different meanings of the notion of a norm (*norme*), the first as an imperative and the second as a rule. On the one hand, Christianity imposed in the long run the idea of an imperious necessity and of a privileged possibility attaching to correspondence; on the other hand, the emergence in the central years of the Middle Ages of a new social grouping of intellectuals promoted the development of a cultural apprenticeship in letter-writing technique.

Sacred correspondence: the New Testament epistles

Christianity introduced to the West a sacred body of letters that was, as it were, already there, canonized through liturgy and providing mediation between heaven and earth, just as the poor man's missive might bridge a yawning social abyss.

The epistles of Paul, written between AD 50 and 65, of which our earliest written evidence dates from the beginning of the second century, constituted by AD 150 Christianity's earliest collection of holy scripture, predating even the Gospels.[3] The corpus was extended little by little and fixed finally in the fourth century to comprise Paul's thirteen letters (the nine letters addressed to the churches and the four letters addressed to particular individuals, Timothy, Titus, Philemon, known since the eighteenth century as the 'pastoral letters') and the nine 'Catholic' epistles: the letter to the Hebrews, almost certainly written by Paul, James's epistle, Peter's two letters, John's three, and Jude's one. The texts by Clement and Barnabus and the 'Letter from the Apostles' are considered apocryphal, even though their claims to antiquity and authenticity are doubtless as well founded as those that can be advanced on behalf of the epistles included in the canon.

The epistles very soon gained an important place in the liturgy: the Marcionites established a parallel between the Old Testament (the Law and the Prophets) and the New Testament (the Gospel and the letters of the apostles). Yet it has also to be emphasized that the epistles retain powerful traces of their initial function.

Paul's epistles to the churches take the form of letters intended for a collective readership, adopting a form of address that is not specifically pastoral and which was to remain in use until the beginning of the modern age: 'I adjure you by the Lord that this epistle be read unto all the brethren' (1 Thessalonians 5:27). 'And when this epistle hath been read among you, cause that it be read also in the church of the Laodiceans' (Colossians 4:16). Paul's tone would become more or less distant, depending on whom he was addressing: 'O man, whosoever thou art' (Romans 2:1), or 'My little children' (Galations 4:19). Yet the edifying aims of the apostle did little to conceal the true nature of the exchange: the First Epistle to the Corinthians was in reply to a letter – regrettably lost – from the said community and it concluded with greetings and thanksgivings that adapted and christianized leave-taking formulas that were common currency in Greek and Latin correspondence. The Epistle to the Romans contains a most revealing passage. Paul, like letter-writers down to the end of the Middle Ages, dictated his letters to a secretary, who might then add his own greeting to the end of Paul's message: 'I Tertius, who write the epistle, salute you in the Lord' (Romans 16:22). In the Epistle to the Ephesians, there appears another figure who was vital to ancient and mediaeval epistolary communication, the carrier, the messenger: 'But that ye also may know my affairs, how I do, Tychicus, the beloved brother and faithful minister in the Lord, shall make known to you all things' (Ephesians 6:21). The envoy (*nuntius*), in accordance with an ancient tradition that extended into the Middle Ages, would transmit orally a part of the message that did not appear in the written document. Giles Constable has drawn attention to the mediaeval equivalence between *epistola* and *nuntius* (the carried thing and the carrying person).[4] The prime task of the papal messenger, the 'nuncio', prior to his representative role, was to gloss and complete the papal letter, to explain the circumstances from which it emerged and the manner in which it might be construed. Many interpretations of decretal epistles need to be reconsidered to take account of the message's irremediable lacunae. In a fascinating article focusing on the correspondence between Augustine and Paulinus of Nola, Pierre Courcelle has demonstrated that the two doctors reserved the written text for the theoretical presentation of their debate, while entrusting the envoy with the task of conveying practical instructions and personal news.[5] Ultimately, a letter might be no more than a messenger's document of accreditation. Henry III of England, on writing to the Count of Toulouse, deemed the perils of the journey at hand reason enough to entrust the whole of his message to the oral memory of the carrier.[6] Nothing specific therefore is to be inferred from the apparent impersonality of Paul's epistles.

The importance of the New Testament epistles derives from this blend of familiarity (Paul writing to his friends) and sacredness (Paul imparting the word of God). The epistolary form itself neatly represents the essential originality of Christianity: the Incarnation brought God to the earth at an ordinary moment and among ordinary people. After the account of what had once come to pass (the Gospel), people disposed of nothing but the simplest of means to pass on the news: the spoken word and the writing of the apostles (literally 'those sent forth'). From Paul onward, there emerged a meshing of communication and of graduated distinctions that continues to characterize the letter-writing norm.

Liturgy of the epistle

The liturgy of the epistle and the contemplation of familiar yet sacred speech dramatizes a form of asymmetrical communication that is characteristic of the letter-writing norm. Very early on, the reading of the holy scriptures became an important part of Mass, and in the West the initial tripartite organization of readings (Old Testament, Gospel and Epistles) gave way to a two-part division (Gospel and Epistles) which was reproduced in the elaboration of the church's distinct sites. The Reading, immediately following the Secret, formed the second part of the pre-Mass, after the Overture (*Confiteor*, *Introït*, *Kyrie*, *Gloria*, collect). The canonical service also included, alongside responses and prayers, a number of readings. At the end of the Middle Ages, the book of hours and the missal brought the liturgy of epistle reading into individual devotions. It is worth taking a brief look at the various stages by which the religious expansion of the Christian epistolary corpus proceeded.

The importance of the epistle increased in step with Christianity's progressive detachment from Jewish forms of ritual. In fourth-century Antioch, the very lengthy readings during Mass were performed in four parts: Law, Prophets, Gospels and Epistles. The Armenian, Gallican and Ambrosian (Church of Milan) rituals included a reading from the Old Testament and two readings from the New Testament. The ancient (sixth century) Roman ritual entailed only two readings, the first of which, on Sundays and throughout the entire Easter period (that is, at just those moments when church attendances peaked), was always taken from the Epistles.[7]

Since that time, the epistles have played a markedly independent liturgical role in the Roman and Catholic Mass in the form in which it became fixed at the end of the first millennium: the letter is identified by proclaiming both its title ('*lectio epistolae*') and its addressee ('*fratres*', 'brethren', in the case of the epistles to the churches; '*carissime*', 'my very dear friend', in the case of the 'pastoral' epistles; and '*carissimi*', 'my very dear friends', in the case of the Catholic epistles). The present immediacy of communication underscores the originality of the Epistle as compared with the Gospel, the reading of which begins by referring to time past ('Haec dixit Dominus', 'in diebus illis', 'in illo tempore': 'The Lord said this', 'in those days', 'at that time'). The reading of the Epistle would end with the greetings used in ordinary correspondence between Christians ('In Christo Iesu Nostro'). The straightforward familiarity of the epistolary dialogue (or pseudo-dialogue) was broken by the subsequent reading from the Gospel. In the Ambrosian ritual of the Church of Milan, the deacon would loudly declaim a warning that demanded respect: 'Parcite fabulis, silentium habete, habete silentium' ('Abstain from futile talk, be silent, silent be').

The difference between the two kinds of readings was underscored by the liturgical attitudes adopted for their delivery: in Rome from the seventh or eighth centuries onward, a subdeacon would read the Gospel from the ambo but the Epistle from his seat, facing the altar, his back turned to the congregation. For in the case of the Epistle, it was the community that was addressing both God and the church by reversing the path taken by the word of the Gospel, delivered from the altar or the ambo.

From the eleventh century onward the reading of the epistle assumed an even more familiar character, with the introduction of musical tropes. In the twelfth century, the call to the faithful no longer preceded the epistle-reading and in the thirteenth century the 'filled' epistle emerged, which interwove Latin and the vernacular.

For every true believer, it was the opposition between Gospel and Epistle that gave the church its spatial structure: the right-hand side of the nave became known as the epistle side and the left-hand side as the gospel side. This layout can be explained: in cathedral churches, the bishop's pulpit is situated to the right of the altar (on the right hand of the Lord); the Gospel is read out therefore on the bishop's side, which, from where the congregation is seated, is the left-hand side. In churches oriented towards the east, the Gospel is to the north, the zone of combat against Satan.

The liturgy of the Mass thus stamped the Epistle with the possibility of communication between God and humankind, while reserving the Gospel and prayer for the representation of transcendence. Meticulous liturgical work has succeeded in providing a picture of the need for a rhetorical technique to establish beneficial relations between the faithful and authority. The epistolary corpus stands at the meeting point between the divine and the human, between the Good News (the Gospel) and the jurisdiction of the papacy, always enforced by letter (decretals, *responsiones*, encyclicals).

Epistolary supplements to Paul

The church correspondence of the Middle Ages acted as a bridge between two highly sacred epistolary forms: the epistle and the decretal. Bishop Yves of Chartres (*c.*1040–*c.*1120), who was prominent in the Gregorian Reformation in France, carried on a correspondence in a very Pauline tone, often verging on the sermon. In his most doctrinal of letters, he followed the opening salutation with a brief sentence that performed much the same function as the 'theme' in a sermon, the Bible verse which, divided and glossed, provided a framework for preaching.

In 1091 or 1092, Yves wrote to the nuns of Saint-Avit, near Châteaudun: 'Yves, by the grace of God Bishop of Chartres, addressing the virgins dedicated to God in the monastery of Saint-Avit in Dunois: how to please the Spouse of the virgins by preserving virginity.'[8] The letter's development was divided into three parts corresponding to the three parts of the initial sentence: on virginity, on Christ as the beneficiary of virginity, and on the means of preserving virginal purity. If one recalls that the technique of division was a latecomer to sermons (late twelfth to early thirteenth century) and that in Yves's time preaching tended rather to follow the patristic model of the homily, this neo-Pauline letter appears to provide fresh impetus in preaching, by applying to pastoral aims the oratorical techniques of Ciceronian composition and of the discourse of persuasion in articulated parts, as this was developing in epistolary treatises exactly contemporary with Yves's correspondence. A century later, the Bishop of Paris, William of Auvergne, in his *Rhetorica divina*, explained the composition of prayers to his clerks by referring to the six parts of Ciceronian discourse.[9] The letter, the sermon, the prayer and papal law all emerged from the same context of persuasion, from a general set of rules governing the word of the church, from a *Panormia*, to borrow the title of a famous collection of canon law compiled by Yves of Chartres from papal letters.

The vitality of pastoral letters, stimulated by the rediscovery of Cicero, was not confined to circles of ecclesiastical authority. Throughout the twelfth century, in both Benedictine and Cistercian networks, letters that urged their recipients to embrace a monastic vocation, developed in short individual sermons, widened the reach of the Pauline message.[10] The epistle provided an extremely influential pattern. While it was true that, with the exception of Hughes of Bologna, none of the great letter-writers of the central years of the Middle Ages ever referred directly to Paul, the apostle certainly did a great deal to give the act of letter-writing legitimacy.

But to return briefly to Yves of Chartres. There are many literal echoes that one might point to: quotations from the Epistles; formulaic phrases such as the one used to round off the greeting to the Countess Adèle of Champagne, 'rectitude and wisdom in Christ', recalling not only the 'In Christo' tag that frequently occurs in the epistles of Saint Paul, but also an expression that occurs in the collect orison said at Mass on the feast of Pentecost.[11] More important, Yves of Chartres's very attitude was derived from Saint Paul: spiritually armed with his apostolic duty, socially protected by his clerical status, stylistically endowed with expressions of institutional humility that chimed so elegantly with the rhetorical straightforwardness of the letter-writer, Yves of Chartres felt free to write without restraint to all the high and mighty, to the Pope, to the Pope's metropolitan bishop of Sens, even to Philip I, King of France. Embracing his vocation, the ministering to souls, Yves carried forward Paul's work. At the end of his letter to the nuns of Saint-Avit, he assumed Paul's venerable mantle in order to command that his letter be granted a public reading:

> I wish and I prescribe, demanding the strictest possible obedience, that once a week this letter be read out in your community, so that you may learn with care to avoid whatsoever is dishonest therein and that you may strive to observe with joy and courage that which is honest and conducive to your salvation.[12]

Urged forward by the Holy Spirit, the pastoral authorized the most daring of exploits and encouraged hope for the most breathtaking successes. Even today, the letter still retains this symbolic superiority over more direct forms of communication. Paul taught (or obliged) the West to believe in the life-giving power of the letter.

In such ways the Christian of the Middle Ages engaged in correspondence between heaven and earth in the firm belief that this would make it possible to reach beyond any mere reading of the Tables of the Law. The full power of the epistolary form was betokened in the extensive and mystical use of the verb *dictare*, which denoted, until the twelfth century, the actual process of dictating a letter to a secretary: 'dictante spiritu sancto', 'caritate dictante', 'dictante pietate', 'ipsa ratio dictat' ('under the dictation of the Holy Spirit, of charity, of piety . . .', 'reason dictates that . . .').[13] Caesarius of Arles spoke of his homilies as letters (*epistolae*) sent down to us from our fatherland (heaven).[14]

Letters from heaven

In the margin of more official forms of worship, communication by letter with the realm of the holy was taken a step further in the letters of Christ, the Virgin and the devil.

The best known of all the letters sent by Christ to mankind was about the inviolability of Sunday as a day of rest.[15] This made its appearance in a sermon by the pseudonymous Peter of Alexandria (fifth century), re-emerged in the Balearic Islands shortly afterwards, was recorded in Rome around 746 and then appeared in a redrafted version in England and Ireland in the ninth century.

The controversy that surrounded this letter in the mediaeval church shows that there was nothing unthinkable in the notion of epistolary communication between heaven and earth. As soon as the letter arrived in the Balearic Islands, Vincent of Ibiza took it as the basis for a sermon, earning himself a stern rebuke from Bishop Licinian of Cartagena. Gregory of Tours believed the letter to be authentic and Pope Zacharias was forced to condemn the act of reading it. In 789 Charlemagne issued a capitulary that outlawed the letter.[16] But this final prohibition scarcely differed from warnings against the Apochrypha, the circulation of which was hampered throughout the first millennium, but took off in the thirteenth century. In the late Middle Ages there are mentions in German texts of a letter from the Virgin[17] and there is little doubt that more far-reaching research would bring to light a considerable stream of correspondence between heaven and earth.

The devil too was something of a writer. The tradition of the devil's letter seems to have been launched by William of Malmesbury in about 1120 (*Gesta rerum Anglorum*) and taken up in the following century by his fellow countrymen Matthew Paris[18] and Eudes of Cherinton. It was not long before it crossed the Channel with Jacques of Vitry, Humbert of Romans, Thomas of Cantimpré, Vincent of Beauvais, Salimbene of Adam and collections of *exempla* (*Tabula exemplorum* and *Stella clericorum*). The travels of the mendicant orders alone ensured it a broad circulation.[19]

The relatively late date of this letter (early twelfth century) explains its rather elaborate form, an approach that was then gaining ground in the fledgling arts of letter-writing. Opening salutations, in particular, were constructed in minute detail. Satan employed the following salutations: 'Beelzebub, prince of demons, in the company of his servants, and all the adverse powers, address their Tartarean salutations and their oaths of inviolate and indissoluble association, to their friends the archbishops, bishops, abbots, deans, provosts and other prelates of the Church.'[20] But it is clear from its content, neatly summarized in these greetings – a satirical denunciation of church abuses – that the letter was designed simply to act as a rhetorical means of turning an argument on its head. These terms of salutation testified to and illustrated a close and special relationship between Satan and the prelates: this form of direct and conscious parody was quite current in the thirteenth century, with the 'Gospel according to the Golden Mark'. In other words, since Christ had put down the pen and Satan had picked it up, the art of letter-writing had lost its innocence as dispatched speech and had set itself up as a branch of rhetoric. This transition almost exactly coincided with the drafting of the first treatise on letter-writing technique, written by Alberic of Monte Cassino in about 1187. The injunction ('write!') was now flanked by a norm ('write by the rules').

The archaeology of epistolary rhetoric

The conclusion that ancient rhetoric, rooted in oral discourse, totally neglected the written word is qualified only by the existence of an implicit rule of social etiquette that in certain circumstances (as nowadays) made it essential to reply in one's own hand, and the shorthand techniques made famous by Cicero's secretary Tiro (Tironian notes).

In the fourth century, however, the rhetor Caius Julius Victor tackled the matter of letter-writing in a manual on rhetoric modelled on Cicero's *Ars rhetorica*:[21] three brief appendices adapted classical rhetoric to the new forms of social life, characterized by the waning of political debate, the bureaucratization of justice and the slump in cultural life. Julius Victor examined training in rhetoric ('De exercitatione'), conversation ('De sermocitatione') and letter-writing ('De epistolis'). The rhetorician's rather perfunctory comments included a distinction between business letters (*nego-*

tiales), belonging to the realm of discourse (*oratio*), and personal or familiar letters (*familiares*), which Julius Victor recommended should be written clearly and simply. A letter was nothing other than a conversation conducted in the absence of one's interlocutor. The passing remarks on salutations (*praefationes*) and leave-takings (*subscriptiones*) foreshadowed the great debates on mediaeval epistolary art: the letter-writer should take account of relations of friendship and rank ('Pro discrimine amicitiae et dignitatis').

Subsequent to this treatise, there is no trace to be found of epistolary rhetoric until the eleventh century – except for an isolated paragraph in a manuscript composed at Monte Cassino in the eighth century.[22] Julius Victor's *Ars rhetorica* in fact marked the end of an old tradition rather than the start of a new one. In the fourth century, letters functioned as poor substitutes for oratorical debate without managing to establish themselves as a genre. In the early Middle Ages, the practice of letter-writing survived and developed but failed to become an independent activity. The archaeology of the twelfth-century treatises should therefore be sought rather in the techniques of administrative formularies, in papal and royal chancelleries.

Cassiodorus (sixth century), a high-ranking officer under King Theodoric and author of twelve books of *Variae*, official letters collected without theoretical commentary, filled an entirely new function, a 'verbal ministry',[23] as cultural intermediary at the centre of the epistolary technique of the central years of the Middle Ages. As early as the fourth century, the pontificate organized a fledgling chancellery which, in accordance with Pauline tradition, legislated by dispatching letters designated by epistolary terms (*epistolae*, *responsiones*, *rescripta*), rather than by those derived from Imperial law (*decretum*, *constitutio*, *auctoritas*). As early as 352, a register of papal letters was created, with value in case law, a distant prototype of what, in the twelfth century, was to become Gratian's Decree.[24]

In Carolingian times, administrative formularies were widely used for secular purposes. Eight groups of such texts have survived to this day.[25] Despite the extreme dryness of administrative language, these formularies, owing to the geographical isolation of human settlements and the complexity of seignoral relations, already betray the general need for a codification of forms of greeting that remained unsatisfied until the production of later letter-writing manuals. The letter, which until the eleventh century was restricted to its conventional notarial uses or to the individual effusions of a literary talent, did not prompt the elaboration of a genre.

The beginnings of epistolary technique: Monte Cassino

The first treatise on epistolary rhetoric was written at the end of the eleventh century by the Benedictine monk Alberic of Monte Cassino. Although little is known about him, Alberic (*c.*1030–1105) was a relatively important figure: he corresponded regularly with Peter Damiani, the monk and cardinal, who was at the centre of the Gregorian Reformation. In 1078–9, Alberic was entrusted with the formidable task of defending the church's doctrine of the eucharist against Bérenger. The fact that he was buried in the Roman church of the Quattro Santi Coronati suggests that he may have been elevated to the curial prelacy.[26]

Alberic left two treatises: the *Dictaminum radii* ('Rays of the epistolary arts') and the *Breviarium de dictamine* ('Epistolary breviary'), whose sequence – which is in fact rather uncertain[27] – appears to mark the emergence of letter-writing as a discipline in its own right. The first of these treatises applies classical oratorical rhetoric to the letter as a written genre. Alberic places 'adversaries' and an 'audience' on one side and the 'writer' (*scriptor*), and the 'reader' (*lector*) of the text, on the other. The divisions of the letter reproduce those of the Ciceronian speech (exordium, narration, argumentation, conclusion). The meticulous examination of salutations naturally replaces the *captatio benevolentiae* of the exordium, while the leave-taking formulas take the place of the conclusion. The second treatise emphasizes the originality of epistolary art and declares that the study of books is a complement to oral instruction. The very plan of the second treatise says a great deal about the nature and likely function of such education: the first part tackles problems of salutation and composition, the second amplification and the third rhythm ('De rythmis'). Although it relates only to hymns, since it forms part of a manual on letter-writing and because of the similarity of the issues under consideration, this final part cannot be clearly separated from the ecclesiastical technique of cursus – rhythmic prose.

The origins of this technique, a feature of mediaeval clerical correspondence, remain, however, somewhat obscure. It can probably be best accounted for in terms of a fundamental phonological shift. In the first centuries of the Christian era, under Germanic influence, spoken Latin lost its classical prosody, founded on the alternation of syllables that, by their nature or owing to their position, were either short or long. As a result of this shift, quantity – syllable length – no longer provided a basis for the stylistic division of units of Latin verse or rhythmic prose, which thenceforth, as in the majority of modern European languages, came to rely on the stress accent. Here and there, the accented rather than metrical *clausula* (sentence end) made an early appearance, for example in the correspondence of Jerome, Ambrose and Augustine.[28] This trend became even more marked in the writing of Gregory the Great, despite the cultural after-image that classical metre had left behind to impede its development. By Carolingian times, a monastic author such as Lupus of Ferrières was unable to tell the difference between quantity and accentuation.[29]

It was not until the Gregorian Reformation that rhythmic prose became an exact technique, known as *cursus romanae curiae*. This was based on the alternation, at the end of sentences, of three rhythmic cadences involving variations in the number (but not the length) of syllables and the position of the main stress. The simple cursus (*planus*) concluded a sentence with a two-syllable paroxytone (accented on the penultimate syllable), followed by a three-syllable paroxytone (—́ — / — —́ —). The slow cursus (*tardus*) had a two-syllable paroxytone followed by a four-syllable proparoxytone (accented on the antepenultimate syllable) (—́ — / — —́ — —). The fast cursus (*velox*) combined a three-syllable proparoxytone with a four-syllable paroxytone (—́ — — / — — —́ —). Peter Damiani, a friend of Alberic, mastered this tricky art: according to Lindholm's calculations, 98 per cent of the clausulas in his letters followed this rhythmic pattern correctly, whereas Pope Gregory VII, a contemporary of Damiani, only managed to comply in 56.5 per cent of cases.[30]

It was not until a little later – under Pope Gelasius II (1118–

1119) – that the cursus was generally adopted in the papal chancellery. It came to act as a mark of pontifical distinction, even a means of authentification, so hard was it to counterfeit the technique. Prior to acceding to the papacy, Gelasius had, under the name of John of Gaeta, been a monk at Monte Cassino, where he had probably been instructed by Alberic. The great Benedictine monastery also acted as a breeding ground and school for the recruitment to the papal chancellery, and it educated another pope, Gregory VIII (Pope in 1187), who, under the name of Albert of Morra, composed an Epistolary Formulary (*Forma dictandi*). From such considerations one is better able to grasp the function performed by the treatises written by Alberic of Monte Cassino, even if the treatment of the cursus appears only indirectly: a form of expertise that was still secret had acquired sufficient prestige for a master to publish an account of those aspects which he felt he had improved upon. There is no doubt that this publication remained fairly limited – though there are manuscripts by Alberic in Bologna. Yet the claim on intellectual authority is advanced very clearly with the mention of an author's name and the titles of a number of rather pompous works. The use made of the Ciceronian legacy was to have more far-reaching consequences than the clarification on matters of rhythm, since the art of the cursus, although not disappearing among the clergy – and even surviving elsewhere, in Boncompagno and Dante[31] – went into headlong decline. The legal and common use of seals in the thirteenth century made stylistic authentication pointless and the difficulty entailed in writing rhythmic prose ensured that it did not catch on.

The church, by inventing epistolary art, had found a way of organizing a vitally important shift in the cultural history of the western world, from oral (metrical, oratorical) to written communication.

Epistolary technique as a social and sociological instrument

Twenty years after the appearance of Alberic's treatises, epistolary technique, with its admission into Bolognese polite society, became secularized. Bologna, in the twelfth century, saw the rebirth of Roman law, providing an exact parallel to the emergence of canon law in Rome. That the art of letter-writing took such firm root in Bologna may be explained in part by its close links with civil law and notarial knowhow. But this success points above all to the emergence of a new class of intellectuals eager to proclaim its political, legal and literary expertise. The preface to Adalbert of Samaria's *Praecepta dictaminum* ('Precepts of the epistolary arts', published *c.*1120)[32] unleashed a critical assault on Alberic of Monte Cassino. Master letter-writers constantly engaged in fierce polemics in which not only social prestige but even their material survival was at stake: students, after all, paid their masters on an individual basis. Adalbert provided a clear idea of the cultural distinction to which he laid claim and which he promised his students, proclaiming that good correspondence combined great simplicity and vast and varied knowledge.

The social aspect of the epistolary standard – as it related to both the writers and to what they produced – became apparent from the start of the twelfth century. Adalbert launched a long mediaeval tradition by introducing a way of classifying the status of those to whom letters were addressed, a procedure essential for the selection of the correct opening salutation. While Alberic, still relying on ancient rhetoric, distinguished three styles – *humilis* (humble), *mediocris* (middling), *grandilocus* (grandiose) – Adalbert sorted letters into three human types (sublime, middling and inferior). The learned Bolognese carefully underlined the social constraint that must guide the writer: he talked of the 'law' (*lex*) that made it compulsory to cite the name of a high-ranking addressee before that of the letter's author.

Adalbert did not reveal the minutiae of his social classification but he did demonstrate the potential complexity of a system founded on two scales, one of which was fixed (ranks) and the other mobile (the position of the writer in relation to the recipient). A clutch of parallel hierarchies (secular, religious, familial) further complicated a model that during the twelfth century would give rise to a whole range of refinements, which have been carefully examined in an important article by Giles Constable.[33]

A late twelfth-century author, Maître Guillaume, constructed a grid that envisaged eighteen distinct social categories.[34] Advances in epistolary art led eventually to the creation of a fully fledged mediaeval sociology which even started to develop an anthropological bent once the need arose to understand the customs and habits of addressees. Thus, in Boncompagno's monumental work, the *Boncompagnonus* (1215), in the twenty-fifth chapter of the first book, which is devoted to an examination of letters of consolation following bereavement, the third section of the chapter describes the different forms that funeral lamentation can assume among different peoples. The section is divided into the following headings:

> How it is impossible to know of all the customs of those who mourn their dead.
> Regarding the custom observed by the Romans for mourning their dead.
> Regarding those who imitate the Romans in their lamentation.
> Regarding the custom of the Greeks.
> Regarding the Calabrians.
> Regarding the custom of the Tuscans.
> Regarding mourning custom in Romagna and in Lombardy.
> Regarding the custom of the French.
> Regarding Spain.
> How the English, the Bohemians, the Polish, the Ruthenes and the Slavs lament their dead.
> Regarding the custom of the Hungarians.
> Regarding the Sardinians and the Barbarians.
> How certain provincials mourn.
> Regarding the custom of the Germans.
> Regarding the custom of certain Saracens.
> Regarding the bliss of priests and clerics in the matter of funeral lamentation.[35]

This is clearly one of the reasons for the success of letter-writing manuals in the Middle Ages: by examining social classification, salutations and subject contents, such manuals made it possible to think of society as a complex and changing hierarchy. Master letter-writers never resorted to the trifunctional model (nobility, clergy, third estate) or to mere wealth as a basis for their categories, nor did they take much account of nobility. Their classification relied on positions and ranks, and if it is anachronistic to think in terms of a hierarchy based on merit, one can none the less witness here the social emergence of the political notion of public good, sustained by the religious parallelism of functions. Such classification, with its battery of model letters and the subtlety of its strategies, gave pride of place to a 'middle' class that was defined negatively to include all those who had neither superiors nor inferiors. Epistolary art, like law, its contemporary and twin discipline, hinged on a form of social stratification that enjoyed scarcely any other direct expression in a world which, from the eleventh century onward, was becoming ever more concentrated and was regrouping itself into *de facto* communities – villages, towns, associations, communes – that were ill-prepared for incorporation into a feudal and ecclesiastical world that knew nothing of them.[36]

Attention was shone on this urban and para-legal aspect of letter-writing technique by the startling predominance of two centres particularly involved in the elaboration of norms: Bologna and Orléans.

The spread of letter-writing technique: Bologna and Orléans

It is worth taking a quick look at some of the outstanding figures in *ars dictaminis*.

Canon Hughes of Bologna, in his *Rationes dictandi prosaice* ('Reasons for the art of correspondence in prose', *c.*1120),[37] expressed strong opposition to Adalbert of Samaria, arguing for clerical solidarity with Alberic of Monte Cassino – although he was no doubt also motivated by local rivalries. Hughes borrowed Alberic's Ciceronian references and his application of oratorical discourse to letter-writing. He introduced a major novelty into *dictamen* by shifting the focus from examples (to be recopied) to generative models (to be adapted). Thus, under the heading 'To a brother', he proposed a cut-and-paste combination of possible kinds of salutation: 'To X his dear brother / or to his beloved brother / or to his very dear brother / or to he to whom maternal blood and affection unite him, Y gives / his salute / or everything that a brother can give his brother / or the affection of a fraternal love / or the service of a mutual friendship / or the gift of his sincerity.'[38] This model, consisting of nine separate elements, generated twenty possible combinations. This combinatory approach, still rudimentary in Hughes of Bologna's work, was carried to its logical conclusion in *Pratique ou usage de l'art épistolaire* ('The practice or use of epistolary art'), written in about 1300 by Lawrence of Aquila. These texts are supplied with a whole armoury of arrows and brackets that serve to indicate a great number of possible variations, not confined to mere salutations.[39] Modern and contemporary treatises, however, do not tread this intermediate path, suspended halfway between rules and examples that can be put to use at once. It is surely no accident that this model-based procedure was the work of a clerical author: the mediaeval church always sought and found a way to render its knowhow explicit, whereas more secular authors strove to protect their sociocultural position by retaining the odd grey area in the techniques that they set out to popularize.

It was in the same period (*c.*1120) that Henry Francigenus of Pavia produced an *Aurea Gemma* ('Golden gem'). This was the first in a series of rather pompous titles (like those by Boncompagno, 'The cedar', 'The myrrh', 'The palm') that revealed the social and intellectual aspirations of their authors. A little later, towards 1135, an anonymous treatise, the 'Epistolary reasons' (*Rationes dictandi*) made its appearance in Bolognese society. Here theory largely made way for practical tips. The Ciceronian model became more explicit, with a five-part structure: salutation, request for consideration, narration, application and conclusion. Then, in 1140, was published the 'Precepts of Bologna for epistolary art in prose according to Tullius' (anonymous); in 1145, Bernard of Bologna's 'Introductions to epistolary art in prose'; then, in about 1150, Baldwin's 'Book of the epistolary arts', which had been preceded by an untitled treatise by Master A.[40]

By the mid twelfth century, the centre of epistolary art had shifted to Orléans where its development proceeded along more humanistic and less pragmatic lines. The University of Orléans had gained a considerable reputation in the literary and linguistic glossing of ancient authors; indeed, the writers of those treatises published between 1150 and 1220 (John of Garlande, Geoffrey de Vinsauf, Bernard of Meung, Arnulf of Orléans) were well known as grammarians.[41]

It was principally from these two cities, Bologna and Orléans, that the discipline of letter-writing spread throughout Europe at the end of the twelfth and thirteenth centuries. Peter of Blois, the author of a treatise entitled 'On epistolary art according to rhetoric' (*c.*1187), sought to introduce his learning into England. Germany, on the other hand, with the works of Lüdolf of Hildesheim (1239) and Conrad of Zurich, followed the Bolognese model, though this began to encounter competition from Florence during the thirteenth century. The first treatise in a vernacular language (French) appeared in 1260, with Brunetto Latini's *Trésor*.

Epistolary glory and social reproduction

There is still no satisfactory explanation for the extraordinary blossoming of epistolary art, and indeed it has yet to be fully examined and inventoried. It can hardly be accounted for by positing a public demand about which nothing can be known. Furthermore, the correspondence that has actually survived appears to owe little to epistolary technique, and in terms of rhetoric there are few striking differences between letters written in the early Middle Ages and those composed in the thirteenth century.

Epistolary art gives the impression of operating in a circular manner, like a technique for corporative reproduction. A good proportion of model letters have to do with university matters (a student's letter to his mother, to his master, etc.); the letter testifies to the acquisition of a skill that justifies the request it formulates. The following is one of the few model letters that Hughes of Bologna included in his treatise *Rationes dictandi*:

> To a master. To X, a very great scholar in the science of letters, a very eloquent man, Y, a priest in title alone, the most humble of his disciples, offers the service of submission which he owes.

> The grace of God was not content, oh master and most revered lord, to make you a peerless scholar in the liberal arts; it has also provided you with a great gift in epistolary art. This is what is reported by an insistent rumour that fills the greater part of the world; this rumour could not persist were it not sustained by truth.
>
> Indeed, through the operation of an incomparable grace, you have known how to teach to your disciples that which God has given to you to know, much more quickly than other masters. That is why so very many disciples forsake the other masters and hasten from all sides towards you, as fast as they are able. Under your instruction, the uneducated are immediately cultivated, the stutterers are immediately eloquent, the dull-witted are immediately enlightened, the twisted are immediately made straight.
>
> This is why I implore and entreat you to show clemency, requesting that your kindness instruct me, I who have only just arrived in your presence, knowing nothing of epistolary art; thus will you receive from generous servants your well-earned rewards, and from he who has interceded on my behalf and from myself an everlasting service.[42]

On a quite different note, an ingenious and amusing discovery by Bruno Roy and Hughes Schooner confirms the circularity of this knowledge.[43] Model letters could act as a kind of chronicle within the world of the university. A professional and personal row erupted between two masters at Orléans, Arnulf of Orléans and Matthew of Vendôme. Contemporary specialists had already remarked upon a number of polemical allusions to one another in the *Art versificatoire* written by the latter and in certain of the Latin comedies composed by the former. Matthew announced in his *Art versificatoire* that the attack would be pursued further in 'reciprocal letters'. Bruno Roy and Hughes Schooner have managed to locate these letters in a collection compiled by Bernard of Meung, though, since they refrain from naming any particular author, they appear to be perfectly normal letters. One of the said letters defines its subject thus: 'A master recommends himself to some pupils and criticizes their master.' Matthew however had forged a letter from Arnulf (whose style could be recognized in Orléans society from the quotations it contained from his grammatical commentaries) that brimmed with presumptuousness and stupidity. Bernard of Meung's collection contained many other texts that were perfectly serviceable and serious-minded, yet this Orléans in-joke clearly demonstrates the important role that such cultural knowingness played in the emergence of a socioprofessional class in the twelfth century.

The direction of masters of epistolary art

This knowingness and rivalry can only be grasped by relating them to the inordinate ambitions that were involved – which can seem quite disproportionate until one compares them to the present-day pretensions of the 'communications' media.

From the earliest lessons in epistolary art at Bologna, Adalbert of Samaria spoke in terms of a profession or of an office (*officium professionis*) and used the word *dictator* (master epistolier), the political connotation of which should not be lightly dismissed. Canon Hughes of Bologna also liked to play with words, straddling the space between rhetoric and politics, defining the letter as the 'absolute discourse, free from the metrical law' ('oratio a lege metri absoluta'), a rejoinder to the famous political definition of sovereignty ('a legibus absoluta'). The constantly encountered words and phrases lifted from Cicero give a clear idea of the social milieu on which the *dictatores* set their sights: the letter was intended to fill the role that deliberative rhetoric had performed in antiquity; its job was to act as a vehicle for political decision-making.

The vast scope of such ambition becomes apparent when, like Enrico Artifoni,[44] one examines the politicization of speech – or the verbalization of politics – in the Italian cities of the twelfth and thirteenth centuries. In Italian communes, from the middle of the twelfth century onward, consular regimes gave way to professional governments led by a *podestà* foreign to both the city and its bloody rivalries (between *popoli* and *nobili*, the old and the new bourgeoisie). The *podestà*, often of university origin, had to dispense good government through the use of effective language as taught by rhetoric – a discipline that had taken refuge, essentially, in the *dictamen* – as illustrated by Brunetto Latini's play on the words *rector* and *rhetor* (leader/rhetorician).

Above all, politics required the mastery of an oratorical art (*ars arengandi*, *ars concionendi*, the art of the harangue or the art of debate) together with the art of letter-writing. All the principal authors of rhetorical-political manuals, Bene, Brunetto Latini and Boncompagno, were master epistoliers first and foremost. Rhetorical technique, whether oral or written, like law, like the *podestà*, played the role of a neutral third party above the fray. At the beginning of the thirteenth century, Boncompagno spoke of epistolary art in the following terms: it was 'by the grace of God, the universal arbitrator of the state, the general mistress of councils, orators, judges, and the empress of the liberal arts'. Frederick II himself, by locating sovereignty in Justice, positioned himself at the crossroads of three sacred types of legitimacy of power in the thirteenth century: the Roman *lex* – the emperor was the embodiment of Law; the natural and divine Justice of the Christian doctrine; and the eloquent Wisdom of the rhetoricians. His foremost adviser, Peter de Vines, was at once a lawyer and a master epistolier.[45]

The triumph of the prince of epistoliers: Boncompagno

A quick survey of the careers of two master epistoliers demonstrates the real practical scope of this social ambition. Boncompagno (*c.*1170–1240) embodied perfectly the success of this ambitious model of the master epistolier, the '*dictator*'. Born at Signa, near Florence, he earned the title of master of arts in Bologna, where he probably studied under the eminent professor of civil law, Azon. He soon returned, however, to Florence to teach epistolary art. This brought him such success that, although he failed to obtain the prebend that he had requested from Pope Celestine III, he achieved civic glory, especially following the publication, in 1215, of his masterpiece, the *Boncompagnonus*. Indeed, this was crowned with laurel during a special ceremony on the Florentine hill known as the Paradisio.[46] For reasons that remain obscure but which testify to his political influence, he opposed the city's consular oligarchy and so, shortly after his triumph, left Florence for Venice (1215–20). He soon moved again, this time to Padua, where he helped to promote the city's secession from Venice. Later on, he moved to Reggio Emilia and thence to Rome, where it is possible that he obtained high office in the Curia. Everywhere he went, this 'prince of the *dictatores*', as he was known, was received in splendour.

With the exception of a brief historical account of the siege of Ancona, his large oeuvre fell wholly within the province of epistolary art, though it also encompassed law, political science and notarial art. In ten or so treatises he covered the whole rhetorical field of the *dictamen*: the 'Five tables of salutations' (1194) and the 'Treatise on epistolary virtues and vices' had titles that spoke for themselves. The 'Breviary' (1203) examined not only the beginnings of letters but also variations that were possible in matters of wording. 'The palm' (1198) concentrated on punctuation, 'The myrrh' (1201) on testamentary provisions, and 'The olive' (1199) on privileges and confirmations. In 'The cedar' (1201), long before jurists took any interest in the matter, Boncompagno taught how to draw up (hitherto non-existent) statutes of association, even though companies of arts, arms and offices (the 'universities', in the broad sense that the word has retained in Italian) had by this time been developing for almost a century.[47]

There was no form of speech or writing that could escape the attention of Boncompagno, who even wrote a 'Wheel of Venus' about love letters. But his masterpiece, the *Boncompagnonus* (1215), otherwise known as 'Candelabrum' or the 'Meadow of eloquence', examined all the genres together in order to construct an overall rhetoric of epistolary art: Boncompagno defined eloquence as the art of correspondence in the presence of people ('dictare in praesentia'). Some insight into the richness of the *Boncompagnonus* was afforded above, with the summary of one section of one chapter of one of the six books, dealing with ways to mourn the deceased, but a better overall picture is given in the appendix to this chapter, which features its table of contents.

It was in this golden age of the Italian commune, before the lawyers discovered how to use their knowhow to best advantage on the powerful (emperors, popes, lords, city tyrants), that epistolary art, the emblematic form of development of an urban middle class of intellectuals, enjoyed its apogee.

The end of a monopoly and the allegorical revenge of Guido Faba

The slightly later career of Guido Faba (*c.*1180–1245) provides a glimpse, however, of how this triumph came to an end, even if Guido, in an autobiographical fragment expertly deciphered by Ernst Kantorowicz, managed to convey a rather clear picture of the social stage occupied by the master epistoliers.[48] Guido Faba began his career in Bologna; having obtained the title of master in 1210, he continued for a time to study law before devoting himself entirely to epistolary art, which he taught until 1240. It was at this date that, owing to his Ghibelline positions, Faba was forced into exile in Siena.

One of his nine treatises on epistolary art, the 'New wheel' (*Rota nova*), written in 1225–6, was no doubt based directly on his teaching work. Although Guido's system was less broadly based than that constructed by Boncompagno, it was wide-ranging and well-organized. The only one of Guido's works that appears not to fit into the *dictamen* framework in fact provided the art of letter-writing with a range of materials: his 'Survey of vices and virtues' presented a collection of proverbs in Latin and Tuscan that were intended for use in the *exordia* of letters. His work comprised general treatises (the 'New wheel', the 'Survey of the dictamen'), collections of model letters (*Dictamina rhetorica*, *Parlamenta et epistole*, *Epistole*), and specialist books on particular aspects of letter-writing technique: the 'Gem of purple', the 'Harangues' and the *Exordia* focus on the opening passages of letters and on the way that they present arguments.

In his autobiography, Giudo Faba recast his life in grandiose allegorical and even directly religious terms. After somewhat hesitant beginnings, epistolary art had invaded him through divine inspiration: 'May epistolary science descend on everyone like the grace of the Holy Spirit.' Like theology, this science, a combination of Cicero and Solomon, had something holy about it: papal bulls were the clear proof of this. Giudo played on the word *littera* (denoting the letter of the holy text and a missive) in order to speak of the 'holy letter' that brought together in one and the same place Bologna and Saint Peter of the Vatican. Faba then commented on his itinerary in allegorical terms: equipped with a solid literary background, he was forced, in order to survive, to work in a forge, where he sustained three injuries, making him lame, blind in one eye and a stutterer. He was obliged to leave the forge, but renounced the tanner's craft, which involved the use of dog excrement to bleach hides and an awl to stitch them together: that is to say, he followed the path taken by Jesus, rhetoric, after undergoing at the forge the Passion that marked him with stigmata.

Kantorowicz has used detailed analysis to show that in allegorical terms the forge stands for the law and the work of the tanner for the skill of the notary. Read in this light, Giudo Faba's autobiography made claims to cultural and social superiority over neighbouring and competing disciplines. By contrasting the man of parchment (*carta*) with the man of discourse (*oratio*), Guido pointed to an intense rivalry that was to end to the advantage of the notaries. Notarial art established itself in Bologna along with the discipline of civil law, in the person of Irnerius, the distinguished founder of notarial art. The profession was very quick to extend its technical expertise (shorthand) to the drawing-up of legal and administrative documents and to the application of law. The master epistoliers were jealous of their strong cultural identity, as expressed in the myth of divine inspiration or genius, and they fought fiercely to defend it. Indeed, the great Boncompagno himself had to submit to the calumnies hurled at him by Bene of Florence. But the notaries knew how to organize themselves and in 1250 a faculty of notarial art was created in Bologna, and then, in 1304, a corporation was founded: the Society of Notaries of the City of Bologna.

It is not hard to see what was at stake in this conflict between jurist, notary and epistolier, even though our present-day categories can cause us to forget that mediaeval societies did not accord law any permanent status. Poised between natural or divine law, which soared high above all worldly powers, and positive law created by the sovereign and very much to his own design, the place of the jurist – and also that of any other specialist in the organization of societies, including the *dictator* – relied on the good-will of the established powers, which accordingly had not only to be convinced but also persuaded to convince others. Intellectuals had to invent the reasons for their own necessity and fight for control over social discourse from broad-based cultural positions (epistolary art), specific administrative skills (the notarial profession) or from consistent speculations (legal science).

Shifts in the formulary illusion

The establishment of the state during the last few centuries of the Middle Ages underlined the triumph of the notaries and lawyers over the epistoliers. From this time onward, communication with the upper echelons of the judiciary or government involved the use of compulsory and complex channels: the initiative of particular subjects no longer counted for much.

An example of this is provided by the sixteenth-century letters applying for pardon that have recently been analysed by Natalie Zemon Davis:[49] to plead for pardon, a man accused of committing a violent crime could write directly to the king, who would then reply. This correspondence of 'capital' importance (the very survival of the defendant was at stake) had to be conducted via the royal notaries or secretaries, who were crown appointees. And if, as Natalie Davis has demonstrated, notaries tended apparently to respect the original accounts of the accused by confining their own input to the choice of opening and closing expressions, the accused, keen to show their statement or confession to the best possible advantage, turned for advice to men of the law rather than to master letter-writers: it was, after all, less a matter of seducing than of highlighting the deeds that could be confessed and the mitigating circumstances.

The skill of the master epistoliers might have proved useful, given that it was they who had inherited the legal legacy of Ciceronian speech (there could be no more eloquent letter applying for pardon than Cicero's 'For Milo' and Boncompagno devoted an entire chapter of his Boncompagnonus to setting out the circumstances of a crime), but from the fourteenth to the sixteenth century the power of the institution and the tangle of legal complexities tipped the scales very much in favour of experts in law as against artists at persuasion.

Master epistoliers accordingly renounced their public ambitions and fell back on the domain of private life, which became the principal focus of subsequent treatises throughout the modern period and up until the present day. Yet it would be a mistake to think that it was during the period between the twelfth and the fifteenth centuries that the art of letter-writing shifted its focus from public to private life. Indeed, the love letter genre developed at precisely the same time as the treatises on epistolary art and certain exchanges of letters, whether real of fictional, earned themselves a place in the collections of model letters as early as the twelfth century. Giles Constable has remarked on the apparently paradoxical way in which extreme formalization of the letter coincided with its increasingly personal content.[50] But these were probably two aspects of the same phenomenon whereby the Pauline imperative was progressively secularized on contact with the newly rediscovered Ciceronian rhetoric. Also, the *dictamen* of the Middle Ages mixed public and private spheres by emphasizing the value of 'friendship' (*amicitia*), understood as a relationship that was freely chosen, as opposed to a relationship of (economic, social or political) dependency, whether by birth or by contract. Epistolary rhetoric, seeking to reassemble the entire legacy of antiquity, aimed to create a new area of discourse, a space between enforced structures. Paul and Cicero had supplied a model of mediation, between God and the believer, between Justice and the individual and, as has been suggested, the effort to produce an epistolary standard summoned into existence a sort of spontaneous sociology of the middle estate. The social history of the master epistoliers engendered the hope that a class of verbal ministers might be created between society's estates. In other words, the epistolary norm had given expression to this unique feature of western history that emerged in the Middle Ages: the aspiration to create a middle class.

There is no doubt that in the treadmill of social rank, where each foothold descends as soon as it is reached, epistolary skill has lost its power of seduction. But the contemporary myth of 'communication' has taken up the baton of verbal trickery. Universities now attempt to teach 'techniques of expression' and a whole 'continuous education' industry makes its living off the empty formalism of communication – and shores up, with the aid of ever newer regulations and imperatives, its powerful role as a social hallucinogen.

APPENDIX: Table of Chapters of the *Boncompagnonus* by Boncompagno of Signa (1215)

How the work is divided

This work is divided into six well-ordered books. The first deals with the form of letters on the condition of students. The second book touches on the form of the letters of the Roman Church, but briefly and summarily, since plenitude has no need of supplementary perfection. The third contains the form of letters that have to be sent to the supreme pontiff. The fourth is about the letters of emperors, kings and queens, and the missives and replies that subjects can address to them. The fifth book concerns prelates and their subordinates, as well as ecclesiastical matters. The sixth book consists of letters from noble and bourgeois men of the cities.

Book one

1 The well-ordered organization of letters
2 Objectives
3 Introductory advice to new students
4 Excessive study
5 The opinions of students
6 Those responsible for students
7 Those who do not take the trouble to reply to their friends
8 The way that many things can be stated in a short time
9 Invectives against those who postpone study
10 Happy events that befall students at the outset of their studies
11 Unhappy events that befall students at the outset of their studies
12 The characters, work and good or bad morals of students
13 Honest morals and depraved morals of students
14 Excuses

15 Honour and disgrace of convents
16 Masters called upon to head a school
17 Interpretations of proper names
18 Those who are misled by stupid credulity
19 Cantors
20 Applications for grants
21 The poverty of students
22 Applications for ecclesiastical benefices in schools
23 Recommendations
24 Dismissals
25 Consolations
26 Customs of mourning
27 Funeral customs

Book two

1 Promotions
2 Excommunications
3 Commissions
4 Ecclesiastical benefices
5 Recommendations made by the Pope for his associates

Book three

1 Letters sent to the Pope at the start of his reign
2 Recommendations of people of rank below the Pope
3 Applications for confirmations
4 Elections made in discord
5 Those who are supplanted in an election
6 Applications to the Pope from people of high rank in favour of their associates
7 Applications to the Pope regarding the practical management of churches
8 General *exordia* to the Pope for those who cannot seek justice elsewhere
9 Entreaties for protection
10 New rumours and announcements of victories

11 Consultations
12 Renunciations
13 Accusations against legates
14 Excuses
15 Obvious impediments
16 Oppressions and wrongs suffered
17 Replies of delegated judges
18 Sentences
19 Abominable crimes
20 Requests

Book four

1 People of high rank send each other pleasant information
2 Announcements of victories
3 Requests made by emperors and kings to their subjects and the replies of the subjects
4 Important issues between crowned people or concerning subjects. Their subjects turn to them about wrongs they have suffered
5 Principal affairs of the empire with the cities of Italy
6 Imperial statutes
7 Consultations and replies

Book five

1 Letters to elected prelates and their replies
2 Interpretations of certain official names
3 Letters to those elected to the head of hospitals and of those houses that are usually headed by laity
4 Letters for those who are elected in discord
5 Those who wish to practise simony; those who consent; those who refuse
6 Persuasion and dissuasion of candidates
7 People promoted who apply for aid or a subsidy
8 Ordinations
9 Those who have to be ordained

10 The distribution of alms
11 Those who are sent on pilgrimage for abominable crimes
12 Priests and monks who receive a permission from bishops or other high-ranking prelates with letters bearing witness to this
13 Those who refuse to leave on pilgrimage
14 Episcopal orders to subjects for weddings
15 Authorizations
16 Metropolitans and bishops command their subordinates to come to synod and to pay a tax
17 Bishops' prattle or other prelates' exactions
18 Requests by bishops for clerks and students, in order to procure ecclesiastical benefices for them
19 Complaints of subordinates; warnings and remonstrances by the higher-ranking prelacy both to lower-ranking prelates and to subordinates
20 Monks, nuns and religions
21 Fugitive monks and nuns
22 Heretics
23 Letters of summons
24 Requests formulated before the law
25 Letters for matrimonial disputes
26 Letters to constrain witnesses
27 Thefts, injuries and fires of which neighbours or servants are suspected

Book six

1 The acquisition of new friends
2 Persuasions and dissuasions in matrimonial negotiations
3 Letters exchanged by friends in wartime
4 Victories, truces and compromises
5 Guards of places and prisoners. Letters from prisoners
6 Recommendations of those who have to become soldiers. Letters of security
7 Tournaments and weddings
8 Jugglers' remunerations
9 Guarantors and borrowers

10 Elections of *podestàs*
11 Applications for compensation for wrongs suffered or for reciprocal wrongs
12 Witnesses
13 Merchants
14 Stores

Notes

1 The collection by Bernard of Meung, of which there are six surviving manuscripts (including Paris, B. N. Nouv. acq. lat., 757) remains unpublished. See C. Vulliez, 'Un nouveau manuscrit "parisien" de la *Summa Dictaminis* de Bernard de Meung et sa place dans la tradition manuscrite du texte', *Revue d'Histoire des Textes* 7 (1977), pp. 133–51.

2 J. J. Murphy, *Rhetoric in the Middle Ages: A History of Rhetorical Theory from Saint Augustine to the Renaissance* (Berkeley, 1974), pp. 194–268; also *Mediaeval Rhetoric: A Bibliography* (Toronto, 1971); G. Constable, *Letters and Letter-Collections* (Turnhout, 1976).

3 All quotations from the Bible are from the 1611 Authorized Version.

4 Constable, *Letters*, p. 53.

5 P. Courcelle, 'Les lacunes de la correspondance entre saint Augustin et Paulin de Nole', *Revue des Études Anciennes* 53 (1951), pp. 253–300.

6 See M. T. Clanchy, *From Memory to Written Record: England, 1066–1307* (London, 1979), p. 211.

7 On the liturgy of the reading, see J. A. Jungmann, *Missarum Solemnia. Explication génétique de la messe romaine* (Paris, 1952), vol. 2, pp. 153–87.

8 Yves of Chartres, *Correspondance*, ed. and trans. Dom J. Leclercq (Paris, 1949), vol. 1, pp. 40–1.

9 See J. Lingenheim, *L'Art de prier chez Guillaume d'Auvergne* (Lyons, 1955), pp. 22–4.

10 Dom J. Leclercq, 'Lettres de vocation à la vie monastique', *Studia Anselmiana* 37 (1955), pp. 169–97.

11 Note written by Dom Leclercq, in Yves of Chartres, *Correspondance*, pp. 14–15.

12 Ibid., pp. 48–9. I have altered slightly the translation by Dom Leclercq.

13 Constable, *Letters*, p. 43.
14 G. Morin, 'Un nouveau recueil inédit d'homélies de saint Césaire d'Arles', *Revue Bénédictine* (1899), p. 243, quoted in Constable, *Letters*, p. 14.
15 See R. Priebsch, *Letter from Heaven on the Observance of the Lord's Day* (Oxford, 1936).
16 See J.-C. Poulin, 'Entre magie et religion. Recherche sur les utilisations marginales de l'écrit au Moyen Age', in P. Boglioni, *La Culture populaire au Moyen Age* (Montreal, 1979), pp. 127–8.
17 K. Burdach, *Schlesisch-Böhmische Briefmuster aus der Werke des Vierzehnten Jahrhunderts* (Berlin, 1926), pp. 22–3.
18 See G. Zippel, 'La lettera del Diavolo al clero, dal secolo XII alla reforma', *Bolletino dell'Istituto Storico per il Medioevo, Archivio Muratoriano* 70 (1958), pp. 125–79.
19 See A. Boureau, *La Papesse Jeanne* (Paris, 1988), pp. 123–8.
20 Matthieu Paris, 'Chronica Major', in *Rerum Brittanicarum Medii Evi Scriptores* (London, 1874), vol. 2, p. 135.
21 Published in K. von Halm, *Rhetores Latini Minores* (Leipzig, 1869), pp. 371–448.
22 Paris, B. N., Ms. lat. 7530, quoted in ibid., p. 448.
23 Murphy, *Rhetoric*, p. 198.
24 See J. Gaudemet, *Les Sources du droit de l'Église en Occident du IIe au VIIe siècle* (Paris, 1985), pp. 57–64.
25 See A. Giry, *Manuel de diplomatique* (Paris, 1925), pp. 482–4.
26 J. J. Murphy, 'Alberic of Monte Cassino: Father of the Mediaeval "*Ars Dictaminis*" ', *American Benedictine Review* 22 (1971), pp. 129–46.
27 Neither the attribution nor the date of the *Dictaminum Radii* are certain.
28 See the seminal work by N. Valois, *De arte scribendi epistolus apud Gallicos Medii Aevi scriptores* (Paris, 1880).
29 Lupus of Ferrières, *Correspondance* (Paris: Ed. Levillain, 1927), vol. 1, pp. 73–7 (letter to monk Alcuin).
30 G. Lindholm, *Studien zum mittellateinischen Prosarythmus* (Stockholm, 1963), p. 10, quoted in Constable, *Letters*, p. 36.
31 P. Toynbee, 'The Bearing of the Cursus on the Text of Dante's *De vulgari eloquentia*', *Proceedings of the British Academy* 10 (1923), pp. 359–77.
32 Edited by F. J. Schmale (Weimar: M.G.H., 1961).
33 G. Constable, 'The Structure of Mediaeval Society according to the *Dictatores* of the Twelfth Century', in K. Pennington and R. Somer-

ville (eds), *Law, Church and Society: Essays in Honor of Stephan Kuttner* (Philadelphia, 1977), pp. 253–67.

34 See C. Samaran, 'Une *Summa grammatica* du XIIIe siècle avec gloses provençales', *Bulletin du Cange* 31 (1961), pp. 157–224.

35 Text published by L. Rockinger, *Briefsteller und Formelbücher des elften bis Vierzehnten Jahrhundert* (Munich, 1863), vol. 1, pp. 143–4. See also the appendix to this chapter.

36 See A. Boureau, '*Quod omnes tangit*. De la tangence des univers de croyance à la fondation sémantique de la norme juridique médiévale', *Au Gré des Langues* 1 (1990), p. 137–53.

37 Published in Rockinger, *Briefsteller*, vol. 1.

38 Ibid., p. 66.

39 See Murphy, *Rhetoric*, pp. 262–3.

40 *Rationes dictandi* was published in Rockinger, *Briefsteller*, pp. 9–28, the *Praecepta* was published by F. J. Schmale in Bonn, 1950. The treatise by Bernard of Bologna remains unpublished (MS 1515 in the library of Graz). The text by Baldwin was published by S. Durzsa in Bologna in 1970.

41 The epistolary school of Orléans, long overshadowed by that of Bologna, has now become better known through the recent work of C. Vulliez.

42 Rockinger, *Briefsteller*, pp. 83–4.

43 B. Roy and H. Schooner, 'Querelles de maîtres au XIIe siècle. Arnoul d'Orléans et son milieu', *Sandalion* (Sassari) 8–9 (1985–6), pp. 315–41.

44 E. Artifoni, 'Podestà professionali e la fondazione retorica della politica comunale', *Quaderni Storici* 63 (1986), pp. 687–719.

45 See E. Kantorowicz, *Frederick the Second, 1194–1250* (New York and London, 1957), pp. 293–307.

46 See the article and bibliography compiled by V. Pini, 'Boncompagno da Signa', in *Dizionario biografico degli Italiani*, vol. 11 (Rome, 1969), pp. 720–5.

47 See G. Post, *Studies in Mediaeval Legal Thought: Public Law and the State, 1100–1322* (Princeton, 1964).

48 See E. Kantorowicz, 'An "Autobiography" of Guido Faba', *Mediaeval and Renaissance Studies* 1 (1943), pp. 253–80, reprinted in E. Kantorowicz, *Selected Studies* (Locust Valley, 1965).

49 N. Z. Davis, *Fiction in the Archives: Pardon Tales and their Tellers in Sixteenth-Century France* (Stanford, 1987), pp. 7–35.

50 Constable, *Letters*, p. 34.

2

Secrétaires *for the People?*

Model letters of the ancien régime: between court literature and popular chapbooks

Roger Chartier

In January and February 1789, at the request of his widow and of the guardian of those of his children who were minors, an inventory was drawn up of the possessions of one Étienne Garnier, a printer and bookseller who had resided in Troyes. Like a number of other Troyes booksellers, Garnier, who had died six years earlier, had specialized in the printing and sale of the kind of hurriedly compiled, carelessly produced and cheap books that, from the eighteenth century onwards, went under the catch-all term of the Bibliothèque bleue or 'blue' catalogue – blue being the colour of the paper used most frequently – though by no means always – for covering these humble books. When they entered Étienne Garnier's shop in rue du Temple, the two work colleagues who had been entrusted with the inventory found that the stock of 433,069 items, ready-bound or in unassembled reams, included 154 dozen copies of *Secrétaire à la Mode*, 73 dozen *Nouveau Secrétaire Français* and 259 dozen *Secrétaire des Dames*. Taking all three collections of specimen letters together, there were 5,832 copies valued at a total of 225 pounds, 1 sol and 6 deniers. The estimated value of each title (not their sale price, which was doubtless a little higher) suggests a hierarchy: the *Nouveau Secrétaire Français* was valued at 22 sous per dozen, the *Secrétaire à la Mode* 17 sous and 3 deniers, and the *Secrétaire des Dames* a mere 3 sous and 3 deniers.[1]

That *secrétaires* were included in the catalogues of Troyes printer-booksellers was no eve-of-Revolution innovation. More than half a century earlier, in 1722, when an assessment was made of the goods belonging to Jacques Oudot, who had died eleven years previously, the booksellers who conducted the inventory at the shop still kept by his widow discovered – surrounded by copies of *Tableau de la Messe*, *Chemin du Ciel*, *Préparation à la Mort*, books recounting the secrets of Albert the Great, Perrault's *Contes des Fées* ('Fairy tales') and miscellaneous books of songs – copies of *Secrétaire à la Mode* and *Secrétaire Français*.[2]

Secrétaires in the Bibliothèque bleue

Surviving copies of letter-writing manuals and bookshop catalogues – such as those printed by the widow of Nicolas Oudot, who ran a bookshop from 1679 to 1718, or by the widow of Jacques Oudot, who was in the trade from 1711 to 1742 – provide evidence of the long-lasting attachment of the inhabitants of Troyes to the *secrétaire* genre. One title, however, not yet mentioned, seems only to have figured very briefly in the Bibliothèque bleue: the *Secrétaire de la Cour*. The only reference to this particular work appears in the catalogue compiled by the widow of Nicolas Oudot, 'bookseller in rue de La Harpe, at the Sign of Our Lady, in Paris'. The three other *secrétaires*, on the other hand, all went through several editions after gaining a place in the Troyes catalogues. The *Secrétaire à la Mode*, mentioned in the inventory following the death of Girardon in 1686, appears in the catalogues of the widows of Nicolas and Jacques Oudot and, as we know from surviving copies, was still being printed in 1730 by the 'Widow of Jacques Oudot and Jean Oudot his son' and, under a licence granted in 1735, by Pierre Garnier. The *Secrétaire des Dames*, the first mention of which in the Troyes printing business appears in Nicolas Oudot's widow's catalogue, was published by Jean Garnier under a licence dated 1759, and a few years later by Jean-Antoine Garnier, his brother, who was in business from 1765 to 1780. The *Nouveau Secrétaire Français*, published in 1715 by Nicolas Oudot's widow, figures in the inventory of the belongings of Jacques Oudot in 1722 and also in the catalogue printed by his widow. It went through several editions: published by the widow of Jean (IV) Oudot in 1744, by Pierre Garnier under a licence dated 1728 and by Jean Garnier on licences obtained by Pierre Garnier in 1736 and 1738.

As with the other titles published by the Bibliothèque bleue, the editions of the letter-writing manuals that have survived doubtless represent only a fraction of those actually published by the Troyes printers to meet the demands of the chapbook sellers. Of little market value, these flimsy little paperbacked books (including and perhaps especially the letter-writing ones) have ill stood the test of time. This explains why, even though we know that these titles had a wide circulation and were reprinted as often as demand dictated, very few have survived in today's libraries and collections. It would be wrong therefore to conclude from their poor survival rate that they did not enjoy broad circulation. Paradoxically, as the numbers of inventoried copies demonstrate, it is, on the contrary, perhaps a token of their commercial success and the intense use to which they were put. But, in the specific case of *secrétaires*, to what kind of use were they in fact put?

Dictionary definitions

First of all, what kind of book is a *secrétaire*? When the first such work was entered in the Bibliothèque bleue, in the last quarter of the seventeenth century (about a hundred years after the publishing breakthrough that enabled the bookseller-printers of Troyes to sell cheaply printed books in huge numbers), French dictionaries made no mention of the fact that a *secrétaire* might be a book as well as a person. Richelet's *Dictionnaire français* (1679) places the term in three contexts: aristocratic domesticity ('*Secrétaire*. He who is employed by some great lordship to write letters and other things'); the judiciary ('The term *secrétaire* is also the name given to the person who records the proceedings of a legal adviser, or to some other prominent member of the legal profession. He who attends to the law-court business of a prominent lawyer'); the plot of a tragedy ('This word is used to mean *confidant* only in Poetry'). The *Dictionnaire de l'Académie Française* (1694) was even more sober, considering the delegation of writing to entail a relationship of dependency: '*Secrétaire*. He whose employment is to write for his master, to make letters and dispatches for his master, for him on whom he depends.'

Only Furetière's *Dictionnaire* (1690) broadened its definition sufficiently to allow for a slide in meaning from scribe to book. The entry for *Secrétaire* established a hierarchy featuring three classes of *secrétaire*, differentiated by status, by the nature of the work entailed and by the social standing of those who required them to write on their behalf. At the top stood the officer in the service of the King, to whom the King's authority was delegated: '*Secrétaire*. Officer who dispatches on the order of his master letters, commands and warrants, and who authenticates them with his own signature' – and in this category Furetière placed secretaries of state and secretaries to the King. Next came clerks in the service of some mighty lord or lawyer: 'The term is also used of the domestic servants of certain Great Lords, or lawyers, who write their dispatches for them and attend to their affairs, who compile the minutes of the proceedings that they are obliged to produce and who warn them when they are able to do so.' On the bottom rung languished those poor scribes who wrote for the populace: 'The wretched scribes who write letters for servants and for such people as know not how to write are called ironically *Secrétaire des St Innocents*.' This mention of a situation in which the *secrétaire* is possessed of a skill not owned by the person commissioning him to write seems to trigger a usage of *secrétaire* as a book which likewise possesses the knowledge of writing which those who refer to it completely lack: 'The *Secrétaire de la Cour* is a book that contains several models of letters and of civilities for those who do not know how to make them.' The title that Nicolas Oudot's widow, by this time established in Paris, entered in her catalogue was the very same as that which Furetière cited in his dictionary. Oddly enough, both associated the 'popular' public that purchased the chapbooks published in Troyes or resorted to writers for the masses with, on the other hand, the epistolary models recommended for use in court circles. An explanation for this paradox needs to be sought by identifying and examining the various *secrétaires* that the Bibliothèque bleue published.

Although the term *secrétaire* to denote a collection of model letters was rarely employed in late seventeenth-century French language dictionaries, the usage was already at least a century old. The work that introduced this new acceptance of the term was published in 1588. Its author was Gabriel Chappuys, its title *Le Secrettaire comprenant le stile et méthode d'escrire en tous genres de lettres missives [...] illustré d'exemples [...] extraict de plusieurs sçavans hommes* and it was published by the Parisian Abel L'Angelier.[3] The work was clearly inspired by and modelled on Francesco Sansovino's *Del Secrettario*, published in Venice in 1569. Prior to the publication of Chappuys's *Le Secrettaire*, the few books in French that were intended for faltering letter-writers fell into two categories: on the one hand, collections of instructions and models that laid out the rules governing letter-writing; on the other, collections of familiar letters that had been handed over for publication.

Formularies and prescriptions

In the first of these categories, the title in broadest circulation seems to have been *Le Stile et Maniere de composer, dicter, et escrire toute sorte d'Epistres, ou lettres missives, tant par response que autrement. Avec epitome de la poinctuation, et accentz de la langue Françoise.* Published in 1553 by Jean Temporal in Lyons and by Maurice Menier in Paris, the book was republished in 1556 by the Parisian bookseller Jean Ruelle in a revised and expanded edition. The complicated genealogy of this composite work has been traced by Jean Ruelle.[4] It borrowed points of advice and letter models from *Prothocolle des secretaires et autres gens désirans sçavoir lart et maniere de dicter en bon françoys toutes lettres missives et epistres en prose*, published by Jehan Langis in Paris in the early 1530s, and from *La maniere d'escrire par responce*, written by Jean Quinerit and printed by the Lyons printer Jacques Moderne. The tips that it contained regarding punctuation and the use of accents were taken from *La Maniere de bien traduire d'une langue en aultre, d'advantage de la punctuation de la langue françoyse, plus des accentz d'ycelle*, written and published by Étienne Dolet (Lyons, 1540 and 1542). Finally, from 1556 onward, classical model letters were supplemented by familiar letters drawn from what was no doubt the second collection of such letters ever published in France, compiled by Gabriello Simeoni (or Gabriel Syméon) who in 1553 had published an *Epitome de l'origine et succession de la duché de Ferrare. Avec certaines Epistres à divers personnages et aucuns Epigrammes sur la propriete de la lune par les douze signes du Ciel* – obviously the epistles that *Le Stile et Maniere* reprinted.

Several different legacies were interwoven in these early French manuals on epistolary art. Firstly, there was the legacy of mediaeval formularies that provided models not only for the letters that chancelleries or notaries dispatched but also for those written by private individuals to fulfil a whole range of social requirements. Predating the great treatises of late eleventh and early twelfth-century *ars dictaminis* – by Alberic of Monte Cassino, Adalbert of Samaria, Henri Francigène and Hughes of Bologna – these collections outlived them both as manuals for the teaching of *dictamen*[5] and as sets of specimens.[6]

Treatises on rhetoric were the second legacy. The titles themselves point to the enduring link between the art of speech and that of letter-writing: 'lart et manière de *dicter* en bon françoys toutes lettres missives et epistres en prose' or 'Le Stile et Manière de composer, *dicter*, et escrire toute sorte d'Epistres'. The oral composition of a letter, envisaged either as the only method of producing it or as a legitimate alternative approach to its being written out in the author's own hand, finds an echo in the frequency with which it would be read aloud by its addressee. Hence the status of the letter as the highest form of eloquence. Hence too the continual borrowing by the letter-writing manuals from treatises on rhetoric. The *Prothocolle des secrétaires*, in its two chapters on 'Epistles' and 'Missive letters', drew heavily on the work of Abbot Pierre Le Fèvre known as Pierre Fabri, *Le Grant et Vray Art de pleine Rhétorique*, written at the end of the fifteenth century but not printed until 1521. Given that Fabri, for the purposes of the said chapters of his work, adapted the most famous of letter-writing manuals of Italian humanism, the *Opusculum scribendi epistolas* by Franciscus Niger (Venice, 1488), it is possible to trace a clear line between the humanist Latin rhetoric and the epistolary manuals written in vernacular languages.

Familiar letters in the vernacular

Parallel to the letter-writing treatises which provided rules, advice and models, another genre was developing: collections of familiar letters in French. Janet Gurkin Altman has produced the first inventory of this type of correspondence – made public by printing and published during the lives of its authors.[7] The very first such collection appears to be that of Hélisenne du Crenne – a pseudonym for Marguerite Briet, a young woman who, after leaving her husband, launched herself on a literary career and in 1538 published a romance, *Les Angoysses douloureuses qui procèdent d'amours*. Published a year later by Denys Janot, her letters, *Epistres familières et invectives de ma dame Helisenne composées par icelle dame de Crenne* are a cross between the account of an individual life and the defence and illustration of the literary talent of women. In 1569 two collections appeared: the *Lettres missives et familières* of Étienne du Tronchet, published in Paris by N. Du Chemin, and the *Premier Livre de Gaspar de Saillans, gentilhomme citoyen de Valance en Dauphiné*, printed in Lyons by Jacques de la Planche. If the publication of the correspondence between Gaspar de Saillans and his wife, given to their son who had just been born, aimed above all to create a shared family memory by according private life so much publicity, the publication of the letters of Étienne du Tronchet, who had been secretary to the Queen Mother, sought to establish a standard. Mixing familiar letters and secretarial letters, first-hand personal accounts and specimens for imitation, letters written in French and letters translated from Italian, this durably successful collection was widely used as a source of models: it went through twenty-six editions between 1569 and 1623.[8]

For about twenty years after 1569, most of the published collections of letters in French were in fact translations from Italian. Acknowledged to be the masters of the various epistolary genres (the familiar missive, the epistle, the love letter), the Italians, through the translations of their letters, acted at once as guarantors and as models for those French authors who sought to demonstrate that the art of letter-writing was perfectly compatible with vernacular language. Although not very numerous, since many readers would have been able to enjoy the original Italian versions, translations did appear with a certain regularity: in 1572, Tolomei's *Epistres argentées* translated by Pierre Vidal and Ruscelli's *Epistres des princes* translated by Belleforest; in 1580, the *Lettres amoureuses du seigneur Jean-Mathieu Adrovandy, gentilhomme italien*; in 1584, the *Lettres facétieuses et subtiles de Cesar Rao*, translated by Gabriel Chappuys, the author of the very first *Secrettaire*, which was published four years later.[9]

In 1586, the same Parisian printer, Abel L'Angelier, published two collections that signalled the return of French letter-writers: on the one hand, the *Missives de Mesdames des Roches de Poitiers, mère et fille*, written by two provincial literary ladies who had also composed poetic and dramatic works; on the other, the *Lettres* of Étienne Pasquier, republished four times in the course of his lifetime. Although it contained no models that could simply be copied out and used, Pasquier's collection, by placing letter-writing in the vernacular at the service of 'moral discourse' or 'matters of state' (as indicated in the title of the third volume of his *Oeuvres meslées*, published in Troyes in 1619), gave the genre legitimacy and set an example that could and indeed had to be followed. There was therefore no abrupt hiatus between collections of familiar letters and letter-writing manuals. Whether by intention or only as a matter of usage, collections of familiar letters formed a storehouse that could be raided for inspiration and ready-made expressions. Manuals, on the other hand – like the aforementioned *Stile et Manière de composer, dicter, et escrire toute sorte d'Epistres* – included sets of familiar letters that were (or at least claimed to be) authentic and that had only recently been published.

Montaigne, however, emphasized the gap separating the formalities of 'letters of ceremony that have no other substance than a fine string of courteous words' from letters prompted by true liberty and sincerity of feeling.[10] Hence Montaigne's rejection of such common practices as the dictation of letters (at the very foundation of *ars dictaminis*, still called *ars dictandi*)[11] or their tidying up after the first draft:

> I always write my letters posthaste, and so precipitously that although my handwriting is intolerably bad, I prefer to write with my

> own hand than employ another, for I find no one who can follow me, and I never have them copied. I have accustomed high personages who know me to put up with scratchings and crossings-out, and a paper without fold or margin.

Hence too, even if he had to fall in line with them, his contempt for the forced formulas of epistolary convention:

> When the substance is finished, I would gladly give someone else the charge of adding those long harangues, offers, and prayers that we place at the end, and I wish some new custom would relieve us of it, as well as that of stringing out a whole series of qualities and titles in the address. In order not to stumble in these I have many times refrained from writing, especially to jurists and financiers. There are so many new offices, such a difficult distribution and arrangement of various titles of honour, which, being so dearly bought, cannot be exchanged or forgotten without offence.

Montaigne, who regretted that he had not been able to cast his 'dreams' in the form of letters ('I would have preferred to adopt this form to publish my sallies, if I had had someone to talk to') and who declared that he was an avid reader of published correspondences ('the Italians are great printers of letters. I think I have a hundred different volumes of them; those of Annibal Caro seem to me the best') pleaded on behalf of epistolary inventiveness and against the formal demands that trammelled the genre: 'the letters of this age consist more in embroideries and preambles than in substance.'

It is hard to map out the precise field of influence enjoyed by the first generation of letter-writing manuals in the vernacular and even harder to gauge the extent to which they reached users of humble background. Yet there is no doubt that the numbers of titles and editions increased steadily: *Le Stile et Maniere de composer, dicter, et escrire toute sorte d'Epistres, ou lettres missives* was published at least seven times, in Lyons and Paris, between 1553 and 1579. It was followed, moreover, by other works that borrowed both its title and its content – thus *Le Miroir de vertu et chemin de bien vivre [. . .] Avec le stile de composer et dicter toutes sortes de lettres missives, quittances et promesses, la punctuation et accens de la langue françoise, l'instruction et secrets de l'art d'escriture* by Pierre Habert, a master writer (Paris, 1559), reprinted in 1587 in a new edition that removed the word '*dicter*' from its title. Then came the series of *secrétaires*: *Le Secrettaire* by Gabriel Chappuys (Paris, 1588), the *Trésor des secrétaires* (Tours, 1598), the *Nouveau Trésor des secrétaires* (Paris, 1614) and, clear evidence of the widespread currency of both term and genre, the *Secrétaire des secrétaires*, and the *Thrésor de la plume françoise* (Rouen, 1624).

Treatises for use by merchants

Specimen letters, moreover, were included in widely circulating works aimed at readers who knew little or no Latin – merchants, for example. Several of the manuals and treatises written for merchants contained tips on letter-writing and examples of commercial as well as other kinds of letters.[12] Antwerp, a great trading city, was the foremost centre of publication for these multipurpose books, which set out to teach French usage, to provide letter collections in two or three languages, to impart advice on business matters and also to entertain. Three examples will suffice to illustrate this. First, a book by Gabriel Meurier, published by Jan Van Waesberghe in Antwerp in 1558 and dedicated to a merchant from Cologne, the *Formulaire de missives, obligations, quittances, lettres de change, d'asseurances, et plusieurs epitres familieres, messages, requetes, et instructions notables, le tout à l'utilité de la jeunesse desireuse d'apprendre à rediger et dicter en François*. Almost a century later, this *Formulaire* was included in a book published in Rouen in 1641, providing in French and English a *Traité pour apprendre a parler françois et anglois*.

Shortly thereafter were published books by Jean Bourlier: the *Stile et maniere de composer lettres missives avec plusieurs Reigles et Argumens, à ce convenable: ensemble obligations, quittances et lettres de change, le tout à l'utilité d'un chacun*, published by Jan Van Waesberghe in 1566 in French only; and the *Lettres communes et familieres pour Marchans et autres. Ensemble contracts, obligations, quittances, lettres de change et d'asseurance, très-utiles à un chacun. Le tout compose en François par Jean Bourlier,*

Troyen: et mis en Flamen par Jean de Heyden, published in both French and Flemish by the same printer Jan Van Waesberghe, in Antwerp in 1576 and in Rotterdam in 1596.

In 1576 it was once again Jan Van Waesberghe in Antwerp who published the *Lettres missives familieres. Entremeslées de certaines confabulations non moins utiles que recreatives. Ensemble deux livres de l'utilité du train de Marchandise.* This book was written in French by Gérard de Vivre, a school-master who had settled in Cologne. This book must have been well received: it was republished by Van Waesberghe in Rotterdam in 1588 and 1597; again in Antwerp in 1591 by Guislain Jansens (who added to the title *Ausquels est contenu la maniere de composer et escrire lettres missives*); in 1611 it was published in Douai by Jean Bogard, who lengthened the title yet further by indicating: *En ceste derniere edition sont aioutés les commencemens et superscriptions des lettres à gens de tous Estats*; in 1616 in Cologne, in Douai again in 1621, and finally in Liège in 1644. Model letters therefore made their first appearance in a particular genre of widely circulating books that were written to provide European merchants with expressions they could imitate and examples they could follow, and that would enable them to get some practice in languages that were foreign to them.

There was another educational publishing initiative, more directly aimed at language study, that found space for model letters. One title among others was the *Pratique de l'orthographe françoise. Avec la maniere de tenir livre de raison, coucher cedules, et lettres missives: Livre très-utile, et necessaire à un chacun, specialement aux estrangers qui desirent avoir entrée en la langue Françoise, nommement à ceux qui n'ont eu ce bien de connoistre la Latine*, published in Lyons by Basile Bouquet in 1583. The author of this book was Claude Mermet, who in the title styled himself 'Writer from St Rambert in Savoy, residing in Lyons'. The book contains three clues that make it possible to sketch a social portrait of the intended or actual users. The title makes a mention of foreigners who know no Latin; the dedications are addressed to the merchants of the author's native city (Saint-Rambert-en-Bugey); and, lastly, in a copy preserved by the Lyons city library, there is the signature of a woman, Andrée Regnault, 'dame de St Joire', placed beneath the six-line stanza printed on the last page of the book: 'This book belongs to me / Who am called by the name below. If any man / Or woman should happen to find it / In exchange for returning it to me / I shall give them for their pains / A barrel full of wine.' A foreigner, a merchant and a woman: the main characteristic of Claude Mermet's reader is that he or she has no love for Latin and does not therefore belong to the world of clerks and scribes.[13]

The choice of Troyes booksellers: Puget de La Serre and the language of the court

In a variety of forms, and whether or not the term was actually employed, *secrétaires* circulated widely in the sixteenth century. Yet the printers of Troyes, when they at long last decided to include the genre in their catalogues, did not turn to the product of any ancient tradition. But it is perfectly understandable that they gave not a second's consideration to one particular treatise – the *Opus de conscribendis epistolis* by Erasmus, even though it had been one of the bestsellers in the first half of the sixteenth century. It had, after all, never been translated into French – as if its educational purpose, with its emphasis on the teaching of Latin grammar and style, had confined it to the school world. Between 1522 (when the first edition authorized by Erasmus was published in Basle by Froben) and 1540, it was republished approximately fifty times, with fourteen Paris and eight Lyons editions. After 1540, however, it was republished less frequently: only three times in Paris and six in Lyons.[14] If Erasmus's treatise was an essential text in the emancipation of epistolary art from the rigid formalities of the *artes dictaminis*,[15] unlike *Civilité puérile* it never managed to reach beyond the limits placed on its circulation by its use of Latin. Designed for the training of a literary youth in the new humanist rhetoric, it was ill-suited for any other readership.

Nor did Troyes printers find what they were looking for in the manuals written by the perhaps excessively professional master writers or secretaries, or in collections of genuine letters, which were apparently too scholarly, or in the books written for merchants, whose publication long remained the exclusive prerogative of Antwerp publishers. Oddly enough, they turned instead to a completely different category of *secrétaires* that had appeared at the turn of the seventeenth century: the court secretary. Cited by Furetière as typical of the genre, *Le Secrétaire de la Cour* earned itself a place in the history of letter-writing manuals in 1625 when the Parisian bookseller Pierre Billaine published the first edition of the book by Jean Puget de La Serre that bore this title.[16] Frequently republished throughout the century, this book had an entry in the catalogue compiled by Nicolas Oudot's widow (in business from 1679 to 1718) and also in that of widow Oursel in Rouen who, from 1692 until 1725, also helped to satisfy the demand for chapbooks.

Yet there seemed to be nothing special to prepare this collection of model letters for the publishing destiny that awaited it. Its author, born in Toulouse in 1593 or 1594, a nephew of a former treasurer of France, Puget de Pommeuse, and a cousin of Puget de Montauron, a financier linked to the Duke of Epernon, was the classic embodiment of a court writer.[17] In 1625 he was still at the beginning of a career that he strove to establish by attracting the attention and protection of the prince by writing somewhat spicy plays 'à clef' (for example, in 1618, *Les Artifices de la court* or *Les Amours d'Orphée et d'Amaranthe depuis trois mois*) or through the allegorical celebration of royal pomp (in such works as *Les Amours du Roi et de la Reine sous le nom de Jupiter et de Junon, avec les magnificences de leurs noces*, published in 1625). But writers in quest of notoriety (and gratification) also had to demonstrate their mastery of eloquence, still deemed the noblest genre, and epistolary art was among its principal forms of expression. La Serre's efforts took various forms: he first attempted letters of consolation (in 1618 he published a *Lettre de consolation à M. de Mayenne, sur la mort de Madame sa soeur, Madame de Nevers* and *Les Regrets de Minerve sur la mort d'Apollon*, a letter mourning the death of Jacques Davy Du Perron), then, in 1624, Pierre Billaine published an anthology that La Serre had compiled of letters written by the most famous authors of the day, *Le Bouquet des plus belles fleurs de l'éloquence, cueilly dans les jardins [...] des sieurs Du Perron, Coiffeteau, Du Vair, Bertaud, d'Urphé, Malerbe, Daudiguier, La Brosse, Du Rousset, La Serre.*

Such anthologies were well received at that time, as is attested by the publication, in the space of only a few years, of collections compiled by François de Rosset (*Lettres amoureuses et morales des beaux esprits de ce temps*, 1618), by La Serre (1624) and by Nicolas Faret (*Recueil de lettres nouvelles*, 1627). They played a direct role in the ongoing argument regarding the epistolary genre between those who supported the *style du Parlement* and those who defended the 'language of the court'.[18] La Serre's collection, like Guez de Balzac's *Lettres* which were also published in 1624 and triggered a vast controversy, clearly indicate the shifts that were then taking place. The site at which eloquence was practised and assessed was moving from the court of law, the precinct of the church or the council chamber to worldly and court society. The form of discourse shifted from declaimed speech to printed writing. The authority on matters of oratory also shifted from the magistrates of the law-courts or the scholars of the Republic of Letters, who sat in judgement over peers, to a public inspired by the taste of the court. The genres themselves shifted from a deliberative style (that of parliamentary harangues or of epistles on affairs of state) towards an epideictic style (paying a compliment, offering a service, expressing gratitude or declaring love).[19]

The *Secrétaire de la Cour ou la Maniere d'escrire selon le temps* exemplifies this new epistolary style. Dedicated to Malherbe, the collection is divided into four parts: 'letters of compliment', 'letters of consolation', 'diverse letters' and 'amorous letters'. In the 1634 edition, published in Paris by Charles Silvestre, these four parts number respectively 60, 8, 29 and 124 letters.[20] The classification is not at all strict, however, for ten letters of consolation are included among the amorous letters and the 'diverse letters' include a title that states 'Letters of compliment and love in the fashion of the court'. None the less, the overall balance of the collection is quite clear – as are its two principal components: letters of compliment, which play on all the registers of court civility, and love letters, the number of which, their interconnection and their imaginary authors and addressees (Silvandre, Clorinde, Hylas) sketch out an epistolary fiction that can fairly be seen as a precursor to the epistolary novel.[21]

Even if one takes into account only those editions mentioned in the catalogues of the French Bibliothèque Nationale, the British Library and the American National Union Catalog, *Le Secrétaire de la Cour* enjoyed a long and distinguished career. Until the middle of the seventeenth century, it was the Parisian editions that dominated: six (1627, 1631, 1632, 1634, 1646 and 1647) as against two in Rouen (1642 and 1645) and one in Lyons (1646). After this, it was the two provincial cities that shared the market: three editions in Rouen (1650, 1675 and a third that can be dated to the turn of the century), two editions in Lyons (1673 and 1713) and, lastly, the Troyes edition published by Nicolas Oudot's widow. The editions that have been identified probably represent but a small fraction of those actually published. This at least is the impression one gains from the (somewhat exaggerated) statements made by the bookseller Billaine, who announced the 1631 edition as the ninth, and by Puget de La Serre himself, who said in 1640 that his *Secrétaire de la Cour*, 'filled with various letters that I had written for entertainment in my youth, was roaming the earth [. . .] with some sort of approval in foreign countries, having been reprinted more than thirty times without ever returning to my hands for correction in the twenty years that have elapsed since it departed therefrom'.[22]

Le Secrétaire à la Mode: editions and additions

The success of *Secrétaire de la Cour* is all the more striking given that in 1640 Puget de La Serre provided it with a direct competitor: *Le Secrétaire à la Mode ou Méthode facile d'escrire selon le temps diverses Lettres de Compliment, Amoureuses ou Morales.* The aim of this new book was quite clear and was emphasized in the foreword to the reader:

> I have wanted to make you a present of this new [*secrétaire*], as of a work in which you will find more satisfaction and fewer faults. It bears the name of *Secrétaire à la Mode*, so that it will at all times be in season, since manners of writing change.[23]

After the first Paris edition, the success of the book was guaranteed by pirated editions published by booksellers in the United Provinces and Low Countries. The Elzeviers of Amsterdam were the first to seize this market: Louis Elzevier brought out a first pirated edition of *Secrétaire à la Mode* in 1640 (with the simple heading announcement: 'Based on the copy printed in Paris'). He reprinted this edition (with the same heading) in 1641, 1644, 1645, 1646 and 1650 and, in partnership with Daniel Elzevier, in 1655, 1662 and 1665. But the Elzeviers were not the only publishers to take an interest in Puget de La Serre's book. Their pirated edition was pirated in its turn, both in the United Provinces (by Jacob Marci in Leiden in 1643 and 1645, by Jean-Pierre Waalpot in Delft in 1652 and by Jean Jansson and Elizée Weyer-straet in Amsterdam in 1665) and in the Low Countries (by Cornille Woons in Antwerp in 1645, 1653 and 1657 and by Jean Mommart in Brussels in 1650).[24] Compared to this outpouring of Dutch and Flemish editions, those produced in the French kingdom cut a rather sorry figure: there was one Paris edition in 1648, published by Jean Gandouin, and two Rouen editions, in 1651 and 1671.

The book gradually expanded during the course of its publishing history. Starting with the 1644 Elzevier edition, printed in duodecimo format, the title read: *Le Secrétaire à la Mode. Augmenté d'une instruction d'escrire des lettres: cy-devant non imprimée. Plus un recueil de lettres morales des plus beaux esprits de ce temps. Et des Complimens de la Langue Françoise.*[25] If the *Complimens de la Langue Françoise* had already been included in the previous editions (in the 1641 edition, for example),[26] the same was not true of the *Instruction* and the *recueil.* By adding the *Instruction*, the booksellers gave their backing to the educational aim expressed by Puget de La Serre, who conceived of his second *secrétaire* as a 'method' rather than a mere collection – like *Le Secrétaire de la Cour.* The 'Instruction à escrire des lettres' with which *Le Secrétaire à la Mode* began pointed out that in order to learn the art of communicating by letter 'one has to have fine examples that one can imitate, and good precepts that can serve as a guide'. The collection of model letters was thus preceded by a series of distinctions and recommendations. The distinctions furnished an epistolary taxonomy that divided the various letter genres into two types: 'business letters' (including letters of notification, advice, reprimand, command, entreaty, recommendation, complaint, reproach and letters offering help or making excuses) and 'complimentary letters' (letters of conciliation, congratulation, consolation, thanks, gentle irony, reply, or letters announcing a visit). The parts into which letters had to be divided were also indicated: superscription, exordium, discourse, conclusion, subscription.

The recommendations were a combination of ancient requirements and brand-new demands. The insistence on 'brevity' and 'clarity' seemed a distant and muffled echo of such lessons in humanist letter-writing as had been formulated, for example, by Justus Lipsius in *Epistolica institutio* (published in Latin in 1591), which enjoined the epistolier to 'brevitas', 'perspicuitas', 'simplicitas', 'venustas' (elegance) and 'decentia'.[27] Propriety (*bienséance*) figured prominently among the new requirements, having to regulate the terms of epistolary exchange according to a precise perception of the positions occupied by the people involved in a given correspondence: 'he who wrote', 'he to whom the letter is written', 'he about whom one writes'. The main thing was to suit the style, subject matter and etiquette of the letter to the situations and persons concerned. As in modes of behaviour governed by strict civility,[28] one and the same formulation can assume a wholly different meaning depending on the rank or connections of different protagonists:

> What would be suitable when writing to one's social equal would be found lacking in grace and could occasion offence if addressed to some elevated personage. And that which is in good taste when spoken by an elderly person of authority would be quite ridiculous in the mouth of a man of few years or humble condition. And one has to speak in different terms of a soldier, a man of letters and a Lady.[29]

Gradations in age and hierarchies of estate set the rules of epistolary propriety. Pertinence or incongruity had no intrinsic definition: the same phrase might be pertinent or incongruous depending solely on its degree of suitability to 'circumstances', that is, to differences in status separating the letter-writer from the addressee.

Three devices were employed in letters to mark the proper respect for differences in social rank. The first related to the amount of blank space left between lines of writing. This applied first and foremost to the external superscription, 'that which is affixed on the outside of letters, when they have been folded, and contains the name and titles of the person to whom the letter is written, and the place where he or she resides'. This requires an expression addressing the recipient (for example, 'To Your Lordship') and, below that, the name, title and domicile (for example 'Your Lordship X / Chancellor of France, etc. / In Paris, Lyons, etc.'). The distance between the first line and the second line had to give an adequate measure of the gap between the social conditions of writer and addressee, and the degree of reverence therefore implicit in the attitude of the former to the latter. Thus, in the case of a letter addressed to somebody addressed by the title of 'Lordship', 'there must be as large a distance as it is possible to make between the first and the second line because one pays more respect when they are further apart.' The internal superscription, 'that which one puts inside the letter', conforms to the same principle: to place a great distance between the title, which is given in the heading, on a separate line, and the second line, which truly starts the letter, indicates the desire to render much honour; on the other hand, to join together on one and the same line the title and the body of the letter is a form reserved 'for those whom one does not wish particularly to honour'.

This immediately visible translation into spatial terms of the ranks and degrees by which the social world was organized reoccurs in the subscription:

> One takes care also when one writes to persons of quality that there be a sufficiently great distance between the subscription and the body of letters that must terminate with such titles as Lordship, Sir, Madam, Mistress on a separate line, removed equally from the preceding text by a small space. Otherwise one leaves no space at all.

Two other features were used to indicate the greater or lesser esteem in which the letter-writer held the addressee: the use of abbreviated forms, prohibited when writing to one's superiors and only permitted with one's inferiors ('When one writes to people much lesser than oneself, and of low quality, one may use abbreviations in the superscription'); the use of the name of the addressee in the internal superscription, permissible only in letters addressed to people of lower status ('One does not place the name of the person to whom one is writing in the internal superscription, except when it is a person of low condition, as when a lord writes to some tradesman').

By the time he published *Le Secrétaire à la Mode*, Puget de La Serre had consolidated his position as a writer. After residing in Brussels at the court of the Infanta, sister to Philip IV (a stay which supplied him with the subject matter for his *Roman de la cour de Bruxelles*, 1628), he entered the household of the Queen Mother, followed her into retirement in Brussels in 1631 and that very same year secured appointment as historiographer of France. In the 1630s, Puget de La Serre broadened the range of his output. He had a good understanding of the various genres of court literature: the accounts of royal 'entrées' (he accordingly became the historian of the Queen Mother's 'entrées' in the Low Countries in 1632, in the United Provinces and in England in 1639); the court ballet, the *roman à clef* (he published in 1630 and 1635 respectively the two parts of *La Clythie or Roman de la Cour*). Even though the 1640 edition of his *Secrétaire* dropped the reference in its title to the court, this did not mean that its author had become estranged from such a vital place where literary reputations were established and rewarded. But Puget de La Serre also turned his pen to an account of the victories of the Catholic Counter Reformation: he nurtered Marian piety (*Les Saintes Affections de Joseph et les Amours sacrées de la Vierge*, 1631), and, above all, he composed numerous moral and apologetic meditations on last days (1630, *Le Tombeau des délices du monde* and *Le Brévière des Courtisans*; 1631, *Les Délices de la mort* and *L'Entretien des bons esprits sur les vanitez du monde*; 1633, *Les Pensées de l'éternité*). In this way, Puget de La Serre's work became emblematic of the connections woven during the first third of the century between the taste of the court and the advance of piety.

In the way it is composed, *Le Secrétaire à la Mode* also expressed this combination of court civility and moral thinking. A 1651 edition (published in Rouen by Robert Doré) opens with a series of 116 letters and replies that all belong to the worldly genres of letters of compliment, congratulation, thanks, entreaty, excuse or reproach. There then follow 22 letters of consolation that are at the same time meditations on death. The collection of specimen letters closes with 40 'amorous letters on all sorts of subjects'. All unravel a genuine plot: the presentation of service, reply, the protestation of love and fidelity, complaints about scorn and inconstancy, the request for a portrait or lock of hair, and the lamentation of absence.[30]

The success of Puget de La Serre's two *secrétaires*, measured in terms of the number of times they were reprinted, cannot be denied. But who read them? In mid seventeenth-century Grenoble, the bookseller Jean Nicolas recorded the name of four purchasers in his accounts book. In October 1647 he sold *Le Secrétaire à la Mode* to a counsellor to the Parlement and, two years later, it was another counsellor who purchased a copy of the *Secrétaire de la Cour*. In 1650 a young lady, a lawyer's daughter, bought a copy of the former title, which was also requested four years later by a lawyer at Parlement. It is a small sample of purchasers but it does suggest, none the less, that in a provincial city dominated by its court of law, the main clientele for the works of La Serre comprised lawyers, and that they also aroused interest in women.[31]

Books published for chapmen: how they were written and who they were written for

At the end of the seventeenth or at the start of the eighteenth century, the main publishers of chapbooks decided to target a broader and more humble readership. This raised two questions. First, whether texts that were read and used by the elites of society were well suited to the lowliest strata in society. And if they were, what special purpose or gimmick might be used to prompt ordinary men and women to go out and buy collections of letters that were thoroughly imbued with court civility, a century or a century and a half after they had first appeared?

A rough outline of an answer to the first question may be gleaned by contrasting three of the editions of *Secrétaire à la Mode*: Louis Elzevier's 1644 Antwerp edition, Robert Doré's Rouen edition of 1651 and the edition published by Jacques Oudot's widow and by her son Jean Oudot in Troyes in 1730. Apart from a dedicatory epistle and a 'Foreword', the Troyes edition contained nothing but letter models, having dropped all the other texts that had filled out the earlier editions. The Rouen edition, for example, had included the 'Instruction à escrire les lettres', the letter models themselves, the 'Recueil de lettres morales des plus beaux esprits de ce temps', the 'Devis d'un Cavalier et d'une Demoiselle, divisé en sept journées' and the 'Compliments de la Langue Françoise'. So the first step taken by the Bibliothèque bleue publisher was to separate out the letters and to reduce the overall size of the work. Whereas the Rouen edition had run to 472 printed pages, the Troyes edition was slimmed down to 146 pages. This determination to cut and condense led to the elimination of some of the letters. Whereas Doré had printed 178, the Oudot edition included only 158. But apart from such abridgements, which sought merely to lighten the work, the Troyes edition faithfully reproduced the earlier editions. The order in which the letters were presented, the way in which they were categorized and the way they were actually written were all identically reproduced, despite the chronological gap and the different kind of readership targeted.

If one opens the Oudots' *Secrétaire à la Mode*,[32] the first surprise is the disappearance of the 'Instruction à escrire les lettres', the educational purpose of which might seem particularly well suited to the needs of a 'popular' readership eager to learn the rules of practical letter-writing. Despite its title, borrowed from the earliest editions, the Bibliothèque bleue *secrétaire* did not provide any of the principles that might constitute a 'Méthode facile d'écrire selon les tems diverses lettres de Complimens, Amoureuses et morales'. The reader, on finishing the 'Reader's Foreword', was immediately confronted with the 98 'letters of compliments' (of various genres) that formed the first part of the work.

This set of letters shared a number of features. First, the world that emerged in outline was a male world: of the 98 letters, 94 were written by one man to another man. Only three were written by a woman to a man and only one by a man to a woman. Second, even if they were extremely short on concrete details that might help to flesh out either the letter-writers or their addressees, the letters that were provided as models did none the less situate the reader firmly within the world of the court. Both of the 'letters to a friend in favour of another friend' were composed to recommend a 'Gentleman of my friends, who is bearing the present letter' (pp.

69–70). The reply to a letter that complained of an overlong absence mentions 'distance from Court' and adds: 'the only way to bring me back promptly is to bear witness to me that I am necessary to you' (pp. 73–4). The collection also contains two examples of 'letters written to request protection from a foreign prince', supposedly written by a 'soldier' who, on the grounds of honour, had violated the 'laws of his Prince' – presumably an unlikely situation for the city-dwelling or peasant purchasers of Bibliothèque bleue chapbooks (pp. 82–4). The relations that produced the model letters were therefore those that governed the relationships between men in court and, more broadly, noble society: the offer of service, the request for favour, recommendation and excuse, thanks for legal assistance, the payment of respects as required by the rules of courtesy, a challenge to malicious gossip, the protestation of friendship. The social world sketched here was organized according to two distinct logics: that of protection and dependency, both entailing obligations and services; and that of friendship between equals, presupposing reciprocal thoughtfulness.

Lastly, the letters of compliment featured in the *Secrétaire à la Mode* were bloodless and impersonal. Full of very general expressions, they very rarely made reference to concrete situations. No one reading them could know what was meant by such expressions as 'the matter that is on the table' that was the subject of a 'letter of entreaties' (p. 29), 'the happiness that has befallen you' that prompted a 'letter of congratulation' (pp. 39 and 40), or 'the mistake that I committed with regard to you' that demanded a 'letter to beg forgiveness' (p. 52). Only in rare cases was any mention made of detailed circumstances which would make it possible to imagine a real situation or sequence of events. Indeed, this only occurred in two letters of excuse: one in which the writer attributed his failure to fulfil his duties to his correspondent to the 'hardship of the prison where I still am' (p. 17); and another, addressed to an eminent nobleman, that began, 'I should like to be left-handed in order to discharge myself of that which I owe you, having unfortunately been temporarily deprived of the use of my right arm. Which compels me to avail myself of another's hand, which now offers my excuses to you' (p. 18).

Puget de La Serre is less concerned to pinpoint particular situations or identities than to focus on the debate between, on the one hand, respect for convention and, on the other, sincerity of feeling – a debate that runs right through the literature of civility. Many of the letters were constructed on the opposition between these two poles: 'So keep your civilities for someone else; and remember another time to act more familiarly' (pp. 22–3); 'Your compliments have put me in a bad mood, I could not write to you but in anger, since you treat me as a stranger by dint of civility in your pointless thanking' (pp. 24–5), or 'You must live from now on with less civility and more frankness' (p. 26). As an antonym for sincerity and familiarity, civility and the formality associated with it were considered by *Le Secrétaire à la Mode* as inappropriate to the style that ought to regulate relations between peers and between those linked by ties of reciprocal obligation. This feature underscored the generally aristocratic nature of the milieu to which the book referred.

The twenty letters of consolation with which the second part of the book begins mark a change in tone. The Troyes edition covers four kinds of situation: a letter addressed to a father on the death of his son, to a son on the death of his father, to a husband on the death of his wife and to a wife on the death of her husband (and, in just one last case, a letter addressed by a husband to his wife on the death of their son). Overall, this series of letters is dominated by male writing: eighteen out of twenty of the letters are penned by men. Somewhat longer than the earlier letters, the letters of consolation belong to a classical genre of epistolary eloquence. The motifs were well-established and rehearsed: the omnipotence of divine will, the confidence in eventual salvation that a life of piety could afford, the need to submit to the decrees of Providence, the urgent need to prepare properly for death in order to secure reunion in the hereafter with the person who had died. The *secrétaire* became a book of apologetics and devotion at the service of a Catholic pastoral rooted in the promise of eternal life for those who led Christian lives while on this earth.

The collection of 'amorous letters on all sorts of subjects' marked a further sharp shift in tone. The Troyes bookseller made no cuts in this, the last part of the book, reprinting in their entirety all forty of the letters presented in the preceding editions. Apart from three letters from a man to another man, which were included here by mistake, the exchange of letters placed the male letter-writer (18 letters) and the lady who replied to him (19) on an equal footing. Throughout the plot that is woven by the exchange of letters, a single theme emerges: the opposition between love and civility, handled by the lover in such a way as to display the sincerity of his passion ('this is no mere recital of civility, my soul shall express to you all its feelings with the same innocence with which my spirit has conceived them, its only object having been your worth,' p. 139), or taken up by the maiden to apprise her suitor of her distrust ('I do not possess such a beauty as might make men wretched or afflicted; so that if you continue with your laments to me, I shall end by reproaching you for it, perceiving your dissimulation rather than your love,' p. 136). As with the letters of compliment or consolation, the style of these love letters seems a far cry from the manner in which any Bibliothèque bleue 'popular reader' might write a letter. One can hardly imagine one such woman reader, for example, declaring to her beloved: 'What do you fear? do you not know that if you love me extremely, I shall revenge myself for this love by paying it back in kind?' (p. 137).

Because they belonged to a social world quite distinct from that of the purchasers of chapbooks and because they took as their examples letters whose style, whether Christian or courtly, rested on the literary conventions of the first half of the seventeenth century, the model letters that appeared in the popular editions of *Secrétaire à la Mode* seemed quite ill-suited to guide the pens of the populace. The gulf was at its greatest between the work of Puget de La Serre, which spread the fashion of the court among the upper echelons of old nobility and the magistracy, and, on the other hand, the letter-writing needs or abilities of the merchants, artisans and shopkeepers, the small country notables or well-to-do peasants who were the mainstay of chapbook readership.[33] For the majority of its eighteenth-century readers, the *Secrétaire à la Mode* therefore seemed devoid of any practical usefulness.

That no attempt was made to define in social terms the letter-writers and their addressees meant that the task of explaining the hierarchy of estates and conditions – one of the functions attributed to the books of civility published in the Bibliothèque bleue – was somewhat neglected. An example of this is provided by the subscriptions, the expressions of leave-taking used to conclude letters of compliment. In about three-quarters of cases (73 letters out of 98), a single expression, 'Your very humble servant', is used. The 'Instruction à escrire des lettres' precisely codified the relationship between the position of the letter-writer and that of the addressee: 'very humble', 'very obedient' and 'most obliged servant' were terms reserved for the most elevated (princes, lords, officers of the crown, first presidents of parliament, etc., distinguished by the title of 'Monseigneur'), whereas 'very humble and very affectionate servant' was suitable for 'lesser people' (those, for example, whom one would address as 'Monsieur'), and the expression 'Yours in devotion to your pleasure' had to be employed with 'those of lowest condition', addressed in the letter-opening as 'Monsr', 'Mr' or 'Maître'.

Le Secrétaire à la Mode does not make it much easier to decipher correctly this set of rules, given that few of the letters actually assume great social distance between writer and addressee. If the expression 'Your very humble and very obedient servant' is used appropriately in a letter addressed to a 'Monseigneur' (pp. 47–8), another letter (wrongly placed among amorous letters) bearing the same opening address closes with a straightforward 'Your very humble servant' (pp. 125–6). There is no foolproof rule of thumb that enables the reader to determine under what circumstances 'very humble servant' should be used, added to or replaced by such expressions as 'very obedient' or 'very faithful servant' ('most obliged' or 'most affectionate' do not occur at all). Left with no explicit recommendations, the purchaser of a Troyes edition of Puget de La Serre's *secrétaire* would never manage to accumulate sufficient knowhow to complete his or her correspondence without making some blunder in etiquette.

The inclusion of rather literary, precious and courtly specimen letters in *secrétaires* intended for the commonest of common readers was not confined to France: it extended to England. The translation of *Secrétaire de la Cour* served as a basis for *The Academy of Complement. Wherein Ladyes, Gentlewomen, Schollers and Strangers may accomodate their Courtly Practice*, published in 1640 and further enriched by the inclusion of model letters taken from *Secrétaire à la Mode*. But, alongside this manual, which was clearly targeted at an elite audience, other titles that were published in the 1680s and explicitly aimed at artisans and apprentices also contained the letters of Puget de La Serre (for example *Wit's Cabinet, Or A Companion for Young Men and Ladies*, 1681, and *The Young Secretary's Guide*, 1687).[34] Even if, in this instance, courtly letters account for only one part of the book, the question raised here is the same as that prompted by the publication of Puget de La Serre's work in the Bibliothèque bleue: namely, how could ordinary readers relate to texts that were so alien to their experience, their education and their requirements?

Before attempting to sketch in an answer to this question, it should be noted that *Secrétaire à la Mode* was not the only book by Puget de La Serre that the booksellers of Troyes provided for their huge but humble clientele. *Le Secrétaire des Dames*, listed in the catalogue compiled by the widow of Nicolas Oudot (active from 1679 to 1718), and later republished by Jean and Jean-Antoine Garnier, in fact consisted of letters taken from *Secrétaire de la Cour*. It was a short book (24 pages) and had doubtless been designed by Nicolas Oudot's widow as a cheaper and shorter version of *Secrétaire de la Cour*, which also figured in her catalogue. In the second half of the eighteenth century, the Garnier editions prolonged, and perhaps exploited, the success that *Secrétaire à la Mode* had enjoyed.

An example of this is provided by a copy of the Jean Garnier edition, published with an approval and permission to print that was dated July 1759.[35] As compared with the book on which it was modelled, *Secrétaire des Dames* retained only a few kinds of letters of compliment and cut down on the number of specimen letters that it used to illustrate each category. The book's title was remarkably ill-chosen, given that none of the letters had been penned by a woman and only two were addressed to one. The different sections into which the book was divided were identical to those of *Secrétaire à la Mode*: letters of entreaty, thanks or excuse, letters prompted by a relation of friendship (to congratulate a newly married friend, to take leave of a friend, to tell a friend of one's forthcoming marriage, to an absent friend, to a friend on the subject of his silence), and letters of consolation. Despite the didactic purpose displayed in its long subtitle (*Pour apprendre à écrire de belles Lettres en langue française*), the *Secrétaire des*

Dames, just like the *Secrétaire à la Mode*, ushered the 'popular' eighteenth-century reader into a social world that was quite different from his or her own, not only because the specimen letters themselves dated back to 1625 but also because the relationships assumed between letter-writers and addressees were those of the court, of the salon or of aristocratic society.

Le Nouveau Secrétaire Français: between tradition and innovation

It is interesting to gauge the extent to which *Le Nouveau Secrétaire Français*, the last *secrétaire* to be published by the Troyes booksellers, managed to bridge the chronological and social abyss that had separated its predecessors from their readership. The title first appeared in a Troyes catalogue in 1715 and was republished regularly throughout the eighteenth century. It was written, however, much earlier by François Colletet, who was born in 1628 and died in 1680. A prolific author of accounts of royal 'entrées', historical journals, descriptions of Paris, poetic and racy plays (for example, *La Muse coquette*, the four parts of which were published together in 1665), Colletet had two titles in the Bibliothèque bleue, both of which were printed in Troyes and sold in Paris by the widow of Nicolas (III) Oudot: *Les Tracas de Paris en Vers Burlesques*, published under a permission dated May 1714, and *Le Nouveau Secrétaire Français*, which rolled off the presses the following year.

In the 'Reader's Foreword' at the beginning of the book, François Colletet clearly stated his intention: to ensure that

> with the aid of this single little portable volume, no reader will remain at a loss, but will discover fit matter, however ill-furnished he be with good sense, to reply to all sorts of missives, and to compose letters, whether to high-placed persons or to his equals or to inferiors, and in a pure or familiar manner, just as one speaks.[36]

This collection set out therefore to be more directly utilitarian than its predecessors, whose origins and, as it were, family relations Colletet sought to establish, emphasizing at the outset the success of the genre: 'There are indeed various volumes of letters, for over the last fifty or sixty years several pens have engaged upon this kind of writing.' This, incidentally, makes it possible to date the publication of *Le Nouveau Secrétaire Français* to the 1670s.

Colletet distinguished between different generations of letter-writers who, 'since the time when the language was reformed', had presented their letters to the public to imitate. The first cohort of such writers included François de Rosset, Cardinal Du Perron, François de Colomby, Malherbe and Jean de Lingendes 'who began to combine eloquence and ease of expression'; then came Balzac, 'who carried it to its highest point' (the first volume of whose letters was dated 1624), followed 'at that time' by Lannel (whose collection of letters appeared in 1625), Théophile de Viau, Jean Auvray, Porchères, Gombauld and Guillaume Colletet, the father of François and author of *Désespoirs amoureux*, published in letter form in 1622. These examples were then followed by 'the letters of Chevreau, of Du Verdier and of a great number of others'. But all such collections could be of interest only to the 'learned' and 'did not teach novices the art of writing about all that falls under our senses, as much for domestic matters as for general and particular ones'. Colletet's approach, accordingly, was to borrow the most useful material from published collections – he mentioned those by Puget de La Serre and by Maynard – and 'to add from our own invention matter regarding everything that occurs daily in ordinary commerce between men'. His intention was clearly practical and his book was targeted both 'at foreigners who are always curious to learn the true ways of our language' and at 'novices' in epistolary art.

In the Troyes editions that Pierre and Jean Garnier published, the full title of the book clarified this twofold, at once utilitarian and educational, objective. The subtitle, *L'Art de bien écrire et dicter toutes sortes de lettres sur les sujets qui arrivent dans la société civile* ('The art of writing well and dictating all sorts of letters on subjects that arise in civil society'), indicated that court usage was no longer the benchmark and that the patterns included had to do with ordinary letter-writing. It also listed all those to whom the work would be 'necessary': 'Foreigners', 'Country people', 'Business men', 'all those who wish to write letters without the help of any Master'. It was claimed, in other words, that the *Nouveau Secrétaire Français* could act as a substitute not only for schooling but also for recourse to the public letter-writer.

However, a comparison of *Secrétaire de la Cour* (in the Charles Silvestre Paris edition of 1634), *Secrétaire à la Mode* (in the edition published by the widow of Jacques Oudot and her son Jean, in 1730) and the *Nouveau Secrétaire Français* (Pierre Garnier's edition, covered by a licence dated 1738) suggests that all such intentions made little real difference to the actual arrangement and content of the letter-writing manual. In the way it was organized, François Colletet's work did in fact follow very closely the two collections by Puget de La Serre. First, the model letters were sorted into the very same broad categories: letters of compliment, letters of entreaty, letters protesting friendship, letters requesting favour or expressing recommendation. Second, when it came to more specific letters, the same situations were envisaged: 'letters asking to be excused for not writing for a long time', 'letters for those who failed to take leave of their parents and friends before departing on a journey', a letter 'to congratulate a newly wed man' or 'to inform one's friend of one's forthcoming wedding', 'the letter from a newly wed man to his brother-in-law', 'a letter to complain of too long an absence', 'a letter arguing one's innocence to a person of quality', 'a letter to an absent friend to let him know of the death of his wife', 'a letter sent to a friend to dissuade him from embarking upon a monastic life'. Not only did François Colletet, as he stated in his 'Reader's Foreword', borrow from Puget de La Serre a certain number of model letters, he even adopted the taxonomy organizing his examples.

Yet there are within this terminology some stirrings of innovation. Colletet's *secrétaire* devotes a lot of space to the exchange of goods and merchandise, the nature of which he details as in an inventory or a sales notice (in 1676, François Colletet had in fact secured the exclusive right to publish a *Journal d'avis* or 'Sales paper'). The thank you letters thus referred to the dispatch of fruit, pâtés, game, bottles of wine or books, and the letters of commission ordered grains or other foodstuffs, books, jewellery, hats or silk stockings. In Colletet's book, money keeps changing hands: it is given to a friend, requested from a charitable person, spent on bribes to win a court case. Objects have their price tag, as is clear from the 'letter of civility' written to accompany the dispatch 'of a lost article that has been found again'. The focus on down-to-earth matters and on the exchange of money or goods introduced new categories into the taxonomy of model letters: 'letters of commission and business', 'letters of papers, contracts and fees to be paid'. While rejecting the flight from social realities that was so typical of the collections assembled by Puget de La Serre, and which had thereby complied with the demands of classical literature,[37] Colletet's book echoed, if not the actual working practices of merchants, at least the concerns of buyers, lenders and borrowers.

The *Nouveau Secrétaire Français* extends the range of relations involving an exchange of letters. For Puget de La Serre, all such relations existed within an aristocratic society that was governed by friendship between peers and dependency on nobility. But in the collection that Colletet compiled, other letter-writing situations make their appearance – albeit very timidly. Some of these were linked to the family: 'a familiar letter from a father to his son who is a student in Paris or elsewhere', a 'reply from a son to his father', a 'letter of reprimand from a father to his son who had wanted to fight a duel', a 'letter from a mother to her daughter who is a nun'. The other letters have to do with relations between servants and their masters and Colletet has three sample letters relating specifically to servants: a 'letter written by a secretary, steward or other servant to his Master to give him an account of the affairs of the Town House or of the fields', a letter for the servant 'to defend himself from a complaint made to his Master', and 'a letter from a servant to his Master to inform him of some accident that has occurred in his household'.

The *Nouveau Secrétaire Français* was therefore, prior to the Revolution, the only title listed in the Bibliothèque bleue that seemed able to respond to some at least of the epistolary requirements of a section of the readership targeted by the Troyes publishers. However, the overall arrangement of the work, the extent of borrowing from previous letter collections and the very form of the model letters, which, even though any explicit reference had been expunged, was still based on court civility, placed it in a cultural and social environment similar to that inhabited by the *secrétaires* that Puget de La Serre had compiled. For the overwhelming majority of its readers, it would certainly be rash to attribute to it any immediate practical utility and, like *Le*

Secrétaire à la Mode or *Le Secrétaire des Dames*, it lent itself to uses that went beyond its declared purpose.

The successors to Puget de La Serre

In the eighteenth century, the *secrétaires* that were printed by the booksellers of Troyes were not the only ones that went through numerous editions and achieved a wide circulation. Two other kinds of *secrétaire* enjoyed comparable success. First, there were the continuations of Puget de La Serre's titles. In 1653, in fact, he himself produced a *Secrétaire du Cabinet ou la Manière d'Écrire que l'on pratique à la Cour* (Paris: Michel Bobin) which combined the letter models included in the *Secrétaire à la Mode* and the various texts that had been added to them since the Elzévirian editions (the collection of moral letters, the 'Specification of a knight and of a young lady, divided into seven days', borrowed from François de Rosset, the 'Compliments of the French language' and the 'Instruction for the writing of all sorts of letters').[38] Accessible, if not new, the book was well received. Its subsequent Paris editions, published by Bobin and Legras (1663, 1667, 1680 – this edition was presented as the book's 'sixth' – 1693, 1700, 1702) appeared to compete quite effectively with the later Dutch or provincial editions of Puget de La Serre's first two *secrétaires* and thus made it possible implicitly to share out the market.

It was in the 1720s that the Bibliothèque bleue finally dropped Puget de La Serre. The republication in Lyons in 1713 of the *Secrétaire à la Cour ou la Maniere d'Ecrire selon le Tems* appears to be the last of his *secrétaires*.[39] The book opens with a text entitled 'Inscription des lettres qui s'écrivent et s'adressent par des Particuliers à toutes sortes de personnes de qualité', which reproduced, but in modified form, the 'Instruction à écrire des lettres' that had appeared in the Elzévirian editions. The judgement as to the proper relationship between the letter-writer and his or her correspondent was still presented as the central principle of epistolary convention ('Care will therefore be taken to honour differently those to whom one writes, in accordance with their virtues, merits and qualities, without however overlooking and scorning oneself, which would be as much a fault as would be to glorify and raise oneself above one's condition, and this judgement must come from our *secrétaire* so that it can be used as we have said').

But as well as this general recommendation, the book also supplied a range of possible expressions from among which a careful choice had to be made. So when it came to choosing an appropriate superscription or opening address, the *secrétaire* enumerated the titles that could be used by an individual wishing to address the king, the queen, a cardinal, a bishop, a duke, a marquis, a count, a knight, a gentleman, a doctor, a monk, a secretary... And, likewise, when it came to the subscription, or closing expression, the manual proposed twenty-one different expressions, arranged in a hierarchy according to the number of adjectives to be placed in front of the term 'servant' (from 'your very humble, very obedient and very obliged, or devoted, servant' to 'your servant'), to the adverb chosen to qualify the adjective or adjectives employed ('very', 'most', 'well'), to the contrast between the concluding expressions (for example between 'your very humble and devoted servant', 'your devoted servant', 'your most, or very, devoted... at your service', 'your devoted friend to serve you', 'your devoted friend'). The small number of forms of address proposed was thus followed by a large range of closing expressions – even if recommendations on their usage were not very precise. This signals, perhaps, the expectation and need for a more explicit and more objective formalization of social differences.

In 1714, there appeared a *Nouveau Secrétaire de la Cour*, followed in 1739 by a *Nouveau Secrétaire du Cabinet*. These were both the work of René Milleran, who had already published in 1690 his *Lettres familières, galantes et autres sur toutes sortes de sujets, avec leurs réponses*, followed by *Nouvelles lettres familières*, which was republished several times at the start of the eighteenth century. Milleran was a keen proponent of far-reaching spelling reform, as was demonstrated in 1694 by the publication in Marseilles of his *Deux Gramaires fransaizes, l'ordinaire d'àprezant, et la plus nouvelle qu'on puisse faire, sans altérer ni changer les mots, par le moyen d'une nouvelle ortografe* ('Two French grammars, the ordinary current one and the newest that can be made, without altering or changing the words, by means of a new spelling [system]'). By invoking, through the similarity of their titles, the authority that had been granted the works of Puget de La Serre, and by drawing new model letters from contemporary authors (Furetière, Boileau, Bourdaloue, Bossuet, Madame de Maintenon), Milleran's collections went through numerous editions. *Le Nouveau Secrétaire de la Cour* appeared in 1723, 1737, 1741, 1742, 1770, 1774, 1776, 1780 and *Le Nouveau Secrétaire du Cabinet* in 1759, 1764, 1790.

Trade letters

The second body of model letters that had a wide circulation in the eighteenth century, even though it did not draw on the publishing experience of the Bibliothèque bleue, was aimed at a very precise readership: traders and shopkeepers.[40] Using and reusing the same titles (*Le Secrétaire des Négociants, Le Secrétaire de la Banque, Lettres marchandes*), these collections had several common features. They were usually bilingual: in French and Italian in the case of *Le Secrétaire des Négociants*, published in Turin by the Reycends brothers (1752 and 1763) and in Nice by Gabriel Floteront (1766); in French and Spanish in the case of *Le Secrétaire de Banque*, published in Paris and in Lyons by a consortium of booksellers in 1768; and in French and Dutch in the case of *Lettres marchandes*, published in 1787 by Vis in Rotterdam. Letter collections aimed at traders – when not bilingual – were often translations. There were, for example, numerous French editions of *Lettres marchandes* which had been published in German by Jean Charles May (one edition in Altona published by David Iversen in 1778, a further one in Leiden published by Luzac and Van Damme in 1780, a further one in Leipzig published in 1792 by Heinsius). Similarly, *Lettres à l'usage des Négociants* was translated from German by J. C. Schedel and published in Hamburg by H. J. Matthiesen in 1782.

The second feature that was common to such books was that many of them had been written, compiled or translated by language teachers. The author of *Secrétaire des Négociants*, published by the Reycends brothers, stated in his 'Foreword': 'During the space of twenty consecutive years [...] I taught the French language with the help of Italian in this Town of Turin'; Palomba, the author of *Secrétaire de Banque espagnol et français*, was mentioned on the title page of the book as 'teacher of the Italian and Spanish languages in Paris'; J. C. Schedel, the translator of J. C. Sinapius's *Lettres à l'usage des Négociants*, was 'master of Italian language at the Academy of Commerce of this Town' (that is, Hamburg).

The third common feature was the inclusion, in proportions that varied from book to book, of formularies that related to trading activities and letters of compliment similar to those reproduced in other *secrétaires* that were not written for traders. In its subtitle, the *Secrétaire des Négociants* published by the Reycends brothers in 1763 listed the main types of trade letters relating directly to trade practice ('waybills and sea police letters', 'promissory notes' and 'bills of exchange') which the book provided, set out in French and Italian alongside the 'most commonly used' letters of compliment 'in each of the two languages'. In some cases, these two kinds of letter might give rise to two separate books. For example, in 1768, Gabriel Floteront published in Nice a *Secrétaire des Négocians français et italien*, whose contents were similar to those of its Turin precursor, and a *Secrétaire du Cabinet et des Négocians* that opened with an 'Introduction à l'Art d'écrire des lettres' and which presented model letters mostly belonging to the classical letter-writing categories (letters of praise, recommendation, entreaty, thanks, consolation, congratulation, excuse, friendship and letters offering a service). The same title and the same approach were taken by Augustin Olzati, a Genoese bookseller, in 1784.

The practical purpose of such collections was undeniable: they provided in different languages, as *Le Secrétaire de Banque espagnol et français* stated, specimens of 'letters of mercantile correspondence for every kind of business and commerce' and formularies that could be immediately imitated. The more ambitious books of this sort could be used as fully fledged trade manuals. This at least was the claim advanced in the long title given to May's collection, published in Altona in 1778: *Lettres marchandes, non seulement fort propres à s'exercer dans le stile épistolaire du négociant, mais aussi à s'instruire dans toutes les parties relatives tant au commerce de terre qu'à celui de mer*. As is clear from the addresses of the printing shops that actually produced the *secrétaires* that were targeted at traders, French booksellers played a very secondary role in a business that was dominated by their counterparts in Italy (Turin, Nice and Genoa), the Netherlands (Rotterdam and Leiden), Germany (Hamburg and Leipzig). Printed in French though not in France, these manuals undoubtedly circulated widely within the kingdom, making it hard for domestic publishers, whether or not they were based in Troyes, to compete with booksellers established in the great European centres of commerce.

Popular letter-writing: deviating from the norm

None the less, as compared to those letter-writing manuals aimed at traders, the practical utility of the *secrétaires* published by the booksellers of Troyes appears less certain. The rare collections of letters written in the eighteenth century by men 'of the people' do little to dispel such doubt. An example of such writing is provided by the letters that a soldier from Neuchâtel, conscripted to serve his country in the Seven Years War, wrote home to his fiancée between 1761 and 1763.[41] The style and rhetoric of the letters and the expressions they use display the greatest possible independence from the patterns of letter-writing made popular by chapbook manuals. This does not mean that they were uninfluenced by any prior pattern but that the pattern should be sought not in the normative and stiff letter-writing treatises founded on court civility but in the sentimental novel. From this genre, Abram Barbezat, soldier of the fourth regiment of the royal artillery corps, borrowed extensively: its vehement and sensitive tone ('Go therefore, dear letter written in my tears, fall between the hands of her whom I adore! Please God that I might have the same fate. Yes, my fate has until now been of the gentlest. But what is to become of me? One of the most hapless! I abandon myself to despair, to sorrow, to tears, but I hope still that I am loved...' (12 May 1761)); its commonplaces ('How happy is my fate to be loved by the kindest lady of the century, I who am nothing and can do nothing. Yes, I am favoured by the Gods who make their devices work between you and me, for one could not find two such tender lovers ...' (26 July 1761)); its clichés ('How very hard it is for a father to be separated from his family and from that which is dearest in the world! But when duty speaks, love must fall silent' (15 December 1762, fourteen months after Madeleine Petitpierre gave birth to a little boy who was registered legitimate even if she was not then married to Abram Barbezat, nor ever would be)).

The letters that Daniel-Henry Jeanneret, a workman who designed printed calicoes and who was also from Neuchâtel, sent to the manufacturers of the Cortaillod factory between 1770 and 1811 bear witness to the interiorization of a rather different pattern.[42] When it came to asking for work, Jeanneret did not turn for guidance to large-circulation *secrétaires* but to the religious rhetoric of supplication that contrasted the humility of the supplicant with the grandeur of the beneficent gesture, accomplished in the view of God: 'If it is possible for you to employ me, I beg you and entreat you, do it for the love of God and not for my sake, do it as a good act and not at all on account of me. I recommend myself very earnestly to your kindness. May it please you in the name of God not to abandon me to my poor and sorrowful situation' (18 October 1793) or 'Thus, in order to shield me and to protect me from such a deplorable state, I appeal very humbly to your kindness, entreating you in the name of God to take a charitable interest and to enable me to obtain work' (4 November 1793). Jeanneret used the Christian language of sin, forgiveness and charity to convey the most ordinary of labouring customs, such as the departure from the workshop without notice or the offer of services: 'If I have had the misfortune of leaving your establishment, I fully recognize and know that I am wholly to blame. It was however through an inadvertent mistake that this befell me, notwithstanding this accident of my own making. I have hopes of your great humanity that you do not want to leave me to perish. There is mercy for every sin. Consequently, Sirs, I beg and entreat you in profound humility to wish through charity to give me work in your establishment so that I am able to earn my living' (7 February 1796).

Far removed from the formulas that the manuals supplied, 'popular' letter-writing managed to develop its own voice by mobilizing a variety of other literary sources. Drawing freely on what they had read, letter-writers could deploy whatever means seemed most likely to influence the person to whom they were writing. Thus, in the two cases cited above, the sentimental novel would provide a handy pattern for swearing one's fidelity to a young girl whom one had seduced and then abandoned, whereas religious pastoral might be more appropriate when it came to soliciting employment from upstanding Christian manufacturers.

Training for the social order?

If one accepts that for many of their buyers chapbook letter-writing manuals were of little practical utility, it is hard to see quite what they *were* used for. They might perhaps be lumped together with books on civility, a great number of which were published in the Bibliothèque bleue, and viewed as textbooks on the hierarchy of estates and conditions that gave society its structure. After all, in the specimen letters presented, the choice of one form of address or leave-taking rather than another was based on a careful assessment of the social gap that separated writer and addressee. In practical terms, what readers could learn from the series of epistolary fictions that were juxtaposed in the manuals was how to decipher a social world in which the legitimacy of an expression, statement or piece of behaviour depended not on its content but on the circumstances in which it was used. By reading letters of a type that they would never themselves have to write, the ordinary readers of large-circulation *secrétaires* could learn the basic rule of ancien régime societies: a correct appreciation of the inequality between ranks was the criterion that enabled each individual to behave under all circumstances in accordance with the demands of the social code.

Yet it has to be acknowledged that Bibliothèque bleue *secrétaires* were not best suited to teaching this appreciation of social proportion. For the most part they published letter models without the kind of accompanying preliminary instructions on letter-writing etiquette that were provided in editions intended for a less 'popular' readership. As a result, Bibliothèque bleue readers were deprived of clear guidelines that might enable them to grasp why, owing to the social proximity or gulf existing between reader and writer, one expression was appropriate and another unwarranted. Further, the *secrétaires* that the Troyes booksellers selected for publication generally represented a socially homogeneous world whose members were linked by relations of equality and friendship. Few of them, as has been seen, devoted much space to letters exchanged between writers and addressees who were separated by a social chasm. As a consequence, the forms of leave-taking that were used did not differ very much and this seems to have severely limited the usefulness of the *secrétaires* for inculcating the founding principles of social identities, based on a proper appreciation of the distance separating self from others.

In *La Double Inconstance*, performed at the Hôtel de Bourgogne in April 1723, Marivaux provided an amusing literary depiction of the distraught embarrassment that chapbook readers might experience when faced with the demands of correct usage. In act III, scene ii, Harlequin wishes to write to the Prince's 'secretary of state' to ask his permission to leave the court in the company of his beloved Silvia. To this end, he engages the services of Trivelin, the 'palace officer':

> HARLEQUIN: Come on, hurry up, pull out your pen and jot this down for me.
> TRIVELIN (*preparing himself*): Dictate.
> HARLEQUIN: 'Monsieur.'
> TRIVELIN: Stop right there! Say 'Monseigneur'.
> HARLEQUIN: Put them both down so he can choose.
> TRIVELIN: Very well.
> HARLEQUIN: 'You will know that I am called Harlequin.'
> TRIVELIN: Easy! You must say 'Your Greatness will know.'
> HARLEQUIN: Your Greatness will know! So he is a giant, is he, this secretary of state?
> TRIVELIN: No, but never mind.
> HARLEQUIN: What devilish twaddle! Whoever heard of harping on about the size of a man when one had to discuss some matter with him?
> TRIVELIN (*writing*): I'll put it however you like. 'You will know that I am called Harlequin.' What next?

So Harlequin proceeds with the dictation. Like George Dandin, quite unable to grasp the rules of civility which the Sottenvilles

(Molière, *George Dandin*, act I, scene iv) struggle to teach him, Harlequin simply cannot see any necessary link between a particular category of nobility and the use of a particular expression. Trivelin, on the other hand, knows his Puget de La Serre and complies with the 'instruction on letter-writing' in the *Secrétaire à la Mode* which specifies: 'One accords the title of Monseigneur to Princes, great lords and officers of the Crown, likewise to constables, chancellors, secretaries of state, first presidents and such like.' With his literal interpretation, like that of Dandin, who could not understand why he shouldn't call his wife and mother-in-law 'my wife' and 'my mother-in-law', Harlequin comically demonstrates his inability to handle a convention which both marked out and transfigured the realities of the social world. It would be safe to say that for many of their 'popular' readers, the lessons imparted by court *secrétaires* on the way society was structured would have remained incomprehensible 'twaddle'.

Unveiling the unknown and social exoticism

One might conclude therefore that the attraction of *secrétaires* of the Bibliothèque bleue lay in the way they represented manners, etiquette and a language that were completely alien to their readership. It may be that the *secrétaires* catered to the same appetite that ensured the lasting success of 'literature of roguery'. It was a market that was interested in lifting the veil on social worlds that were picturesque to the extent that they were foreign to the experience of these tradesmen, artisans and peasants who made up the bulk of the clientele of the Troyes booksellers and their emulators.[43]

At one extreme there was the monarchy of Argot, with its secret language (its *jargon*), its rites and its hierarchy, and at the opposite extreme there was court society, with its conventions, usages and polished manners of speaking and writing. These two milieux lent themselves to a similar interpretation, informed not by any acknowledgement of similarity or any desire to ape, but by a curiosity aroused by the very distance that separated them from the reader. To read a *secrétaire* was to commit an imaginary offence of breaking and entering into a distant, closed and separate aristocratic world. Collections of model letters published in the Bibliothèque bleue, far from teaching the readers about the ordering of society so that they could discover their rightful place and adopt appropriate behaviour, were really part of that broad range of social exoticism that existed in the Bibliothèque bleue collection. Many successful genres – not just the literature of roguery but also descriptions of working practices or details of Parisian life – used as their starting point the unveiling of circumstances that most of their readers knew very little about.

Towards the epistolary novel

But the Bibliothèque bleue *secrétaires* could also be read as stories. Collections of love letters and epistolary novels were close cousins. In a rudimentary form, the letter-writing manual assembled all the essential features of fiction: the unfolding of a plot, the creation of a time-frame and the sketching-in of characters. An example of this is the 'Lettres d'amour sur toutes sortes de sujets' that constituted the closing section of the edition of *Secrétaire à la Mode* published by widow Oudot and her son in 1730. From the 'first letter of representation of service' to the 'letter to ask a mistress for a lock of her hair' and the following positive reply, all the model letters collected can be read as part of a single exchange, unfolding the story of an amorous conquest. The demands of the genre (for example the inclusion of several examples of each kind of letter) assume a wholly new significance: they underline the strength of attachment, the repetition of a particular undertaking and of a particular request for reciprocity.

Likewise, the different categories of letters supplied for imitation are drawn together to form the story of a love that is at first thwarted but then requited. At the outset the plot develops from the resistance of the young girl who is subject to her parents' authority ('being under the servitude of a father and mother, who do not even give me the freedom to write to you', p. 138). Also, she is uncertain of the sincerity of her lover ('You know well that I am in no mood to set much store by the complaints of lovers, given that they die so many times every day in word and yet are in appearance not ill, so that the account of their sufferings comes to seem a fable,' p. 135). Her separation from her lover becomes a decisive trial ('The pains of love are so easy to heal that I never console anyone who is suffering from them. If you are laid low, my long absence, which you now complain of, will soon provide the remedy. If, however, this remedy fails to work, that will still be to your advantage, giving me finally to know the truth of your love by the length of your constancy,' pp. 134–5). The turning point in the story is the lover's revolt, expressed in a 'letter of complaint regarding scorn': 'I have to confess that I am very unhappy indeed that in the three years of my services to you I have never succeeded in deserving that you should say to me merely that they have been pleasing to you' (p. 142). After a final accusation of betrayal, this time turned against the young girl, who clears herself of blame by invoking 'what a tyrannical father can do to a young girl who is in his power' (p. 149), the 'novel' concludes with feminine surrender, symbolized by the dispatch of a portrait and then, an even stronger undertaking, that of a 'bracelet of hair' enclosed in a final letter in which the young girl writes: 'It is sufficient for me to remind you that as these are uncommon favours, they require first of all faithful secrecy on the part of all those who receive them and I think that you will keep them inviolate' (p. 153). The *secrétaire* finishes on this note, shrouding the destiny of the epistolary lovers who have at last been brought together in the secrecy of a story that is not to be related any further.

The reader's imagination is called upon not only to complete the account but also to add some depth to heroes about whom nothing is said, beyond their feelings, and to fill in the silent passages in a plot that never goes into any detail about its development. The only clues the readers are given have to do with the amount of time that elapses between letters. This is occasionally specified (as in the young man's mention of the 'three years of service' he had rendered to his mistress) but more often it remains indeterminate, with references to the patience required in order to face the 'long absence' of the beloved or to comply with convention. To turn the love letters published in *Secrétaire à la Mode* into a story fit for a novel, the reader has to imagine a great deal and to some extent write in the mind an account that fleshes out the skeleton situations that the book presents. But is not that precisely one of the essential characteristics of the various texts that make up large-circulation literature and the 'popular' library? Quite apart from – and even prior to – the Bibliothèque bleue, many of the 'occasional' works published in the sixteenth and seventeenth centuries similarly called on their readers not only to complete the narrative but also to imagine missing episodes or to breathe life into characters that were barely pencilled in.[44] Bibliothèque bleue *secrétaires* lent themselves to this interpretation not only because the sequence of letters in certain of their sections immediately conjured up a story but also because each model letter, taken on its own, could provide the basis for a fiction that its reader could imagine.

Letter-writing manuals might serve to inculcate the principles of a society of orders and estates, they might constitute a literature of disclosure and social exoticism, or they might be embryonic epistolary novels. All such hypotheses seek to account for a type of reading that, in the vast majority of cases, could hardly have been motivated by its practical utility. Each hypothesis sets out one of the relationships that might be entered into by 'popular' readers with the works that the Troyes booksellers so plentifully supplied. Yet none of them fully dispels the haze that surrounds this strange encounter between a literature of the court (or, at least, an aristocratic and worldly literature), the chapbook library and the expectations of readers who bought the *secrétaires* without for all that becoming letter-writers, and certainly not letter-writers respecting the conventions of the letter-writing art. The way in which they understood these texts, the uses to which they put the books of Puget de La Serre once they had become Bibliothèque bleue books and the pleasures they derived from their reading remain largely inaccessible to our historical curiosity.

The nineteenth century: new needs, new readers

By the early nineteenth century there was already some dissatisfaction with books that, though designed for a practical purpose, were of little actual use to the majority of their purchasers. It was this that led to a new generation of manuals that sought to make a clean break with old *secrétaires*, mainly distributed by the Bibliothèque bleue. The foreword to the *Nouveau*

Secrétaire Français published by Le Prieur in Paris in 1804 pointed out that:

> Several works of this kind have already been published but we have to admit that not one of them really achieves its goal. For roughly the last one hundred and fifty years, the best known and most widely available has been the *Secrétaire de la Cour et du Cabinet* by Puget de La Serre, the very same La Serre that Boileau so rightly poked fun at. It is hard to imagine the twaddle that this man could coolly pass off as expressions of *bel usage*. What seems even more inconceivable is that the ignorance of booksellers has perpetuated right down to our own days, with one reprint after another, this miserable collection.

In a note, the *Nouveau Secrétaire Français* adds: 'The style of these letters is so extraordinary that I cannot withold from myself the pleasure of quoting a few fragments – to amuse the reader.' At this point the text gives three examples from the love letters, before concluding: 'and that was reprinted for one hundred and fifty years as a model!'[45]

Puget de La Serre and the numerous republications of his work were thus discredited on three fronts. First by literary authority, embodied by Boileau who, in his *Satires* and his *Épitres*, repeatedly ridiculed a man whose literary career had extended well beyond 1640 in a variety of genres: eulogies and panegyrics, portraits and parallels, tragedy and tragi-comedy. Boileau was convinced that the work of Puget de La Serre was marked out for one of two possible fates. Either, as in *Satire IX* (lines 65–72), it would sink without trace:

> Mais combien d'écrivains, d'abord si bien reçus,
> Sont de ce fol espoir honteusement déçus!
> Combien, pour quelques mois, out vu fleurir leur livre,
> Dont les vers en paquet se vendent à la livre!
> Vous pourrez voir, un temps, vos écrits estimés
> Courir de main en main par la ville semés;
> Puis de là tout poudreux, ignorés sur la terre
> Suivre chez l'épicier Neuf-Germain et La Serre . . .

> (Yet how many writers, at first so well received, are shamefully disappointed by such foolish hope! How many are there who have

seen their book flourish for a few months but whose verses are now sold off in poundweight packets! You may see a while your highly valued writings strewn around town, rushed from hand to hand; but later, gathering dust, neglected on the ground, following Neuf-Germain and La Serre on their way to the grocer's.)

or, as in *Satire III* (lines 174–7), it would win eulogies from the ignorant:

Quand un des campagnards relevant sa moustache,
Et son feutre à grands poils ombragé d'un panache,
Impose à tous silence, et d'un ton de docteur:
Morbleu! dit-il, La Serre est un charmant auteur!
Ses vers sont d'un beau style, et sa prose est coulante.

(When one of the rustics, lifting his moustache and his long-haired hat shaded by a tufted plume, calls on all to be silent and with professorial tone: 'By gad!' says he, 'La Serre is a charming writer! His verses are of a fine style and his prose is flowing.')

Secondly, La Serre was disqualified on the grounds of his outlandishness, the 'twaddle' of a style that was totally at odds with the function of a letter-writing manual, that is, 'to compose simple letters just like those that one writes in the customary dealings of life'. Lastly, the *secrétaires* compiled by La Serre and his imitators were discredited by their inappropriateness for teaching purposes: 'It goes without saying that similar model letters will never serve to educate any of those for whom they are intended.'

This explains the approach adopted by the *Nouveau Secrétaire Français*, which was primarily designed to be of practical utility. On the one hand, it was vital to present usable models: 'We have composed letters to fit all the principal circumstances in which one is obliged to write, so that everyone may find something of interest.' The lengthy title groups these 'circumstances' under five headings: letters for *fêtes*, birthdays and New Year's Days; letters of congratulations, condolence, etc.; letters from children to their parents; love letters and letters proposing marriage, etc.; and business and commercial letters, to which were added models of petitions, promissory notes, letters of exchange and bills. On the other hand, in order fully to achieve its goal a *secrétaire* had to be well suited to the skills and needs of its users, identified here as two groups: children and adolescents and the uneducated.

> The letter models that we present here are principally intended for young people who are not yet accustomed to the world, and for people who, having had the ill fortune to receive no education, sometimes find themselves in difficulty when it comes to fulfilling certain obligations that society imposes and with which one cannot dispense without appearing impolite and uncouth.

The *secrétaire* is thus clearly intended to fulfil an educational and cultivating mission and to instruct those who have not – as yet – gained the necessary knowhow to master the conventions of social intercourse.

Throughout the first four decades of the nineteenth century, the general title *Nouveau Secrétaire Français* covered many different publications which, including reprints, variants and additions, formed a sizable corpus of new letter-writing manuals. Despite the similarity of the title, these works could in no sense be described as late editions of François Colletet's *secrétaire* published in the eighteenth century by the Troyes booksellers. The letter models that they presented were different or differently arranged. The *Nouveau Secrétaire Français* that Moronval published in 1827 thus presented 'model letters for the New Year, for *Fêtes*, Congratulations and Condolences, Thanks, Business, Trade and Recommendation'.[46] The main body of the work was dominated by three kinds of letters, accounting for 29, 20 and 29 specimens respectively (out of a total of 111): first, letters dictated by the nature of the requirement to write them (for the New Year, to wish someone a happy *fête*); second, business letters and models of letters of exchange, promissory notes, invoices and receipts, certificates of apprenticeship and consignment notes; third, 'letters on diverse subjects'. These last letters display clearly the new epistolary order. There is a greater willingness to introduce popular letter-writers (a cook writing to her mother, a sales assistant looking for a job, a wet-nurse writing to her nursling's father, a servant appealing to his master). They also reveal the most usual kind of relationship obtaining between letter-writers and civil servants (for example by providing a model letter for applying to a mayor or to a clerk for a birth certificate or for a copy of a marriage or death certificate). By supplying models of marriage, birth and burial announcements, they also demonstrate how often reliance was placed on printed forms. Without altogether abandoning the traditional expressions used in letters of congratulation, this new generation of *secrétaires* considerably broadened the range of possible letter types, letter-writers and the kinds of situations that could prompt the writing of a letter.

Their success was indisputable: for the period between 1804 and 1849, the Bibliothèque Nationale collection alone keeps forty-seven widely varying editions of *Nouveau Secrétaire Français*, printed by twenty-four different publishers in fourteen different towns and cities. The new *secrétaires* replaced not only the titles that, published during the Revolution and under the Empire, had sought to echo the country's new political direction but also those that had rolled off the Troyes presses during the Restoration. Neither *Le Secrétaire des Républicains* nor *Le Secrétaire de la Cour impériale de France*, both of which were published in Paris by Barba, in 1793 and 1811 respectively, survived the circumstances that led to their composition. The republican simplifications contained in the former, which recommended the universal usage of the familiar 'tu' form and of the expression 'salut et fraternité' (greetings and fraternity) as the only form of superscription, and the respect for imperial protocol contained in the latter, which regulated expressions of epistolary politesse in accordance with the new political hierarchy, very quickly rendered both titles completely obsolete, thus leaving the way open for new kinds of letter-writing manuals.[47]

The Troyes booksellers were unable or did not know how to dominate this new market. That they had a clear idea of the new demands and the new readerships is demonstrated, however, by the three books they published at the start of the nineteenth century containing model letters: *La Nouvelle Science des gens de campagne*, published by widow André in 1823, which included ten model letters; *Le Secrétaire des braves à l'usage des militaires*, printed in Troyes by Mme Garnier and sold in Paris by Caillot, mentioned in the *Bibliographie de la France* in March 1827; and lastly *Les Nouveaux Complimens et Lettres pour le jour de l'An, adressés aux Pères, Mères, Bons Papas, Bonnes Mamans, Oncles,*

Tantes, Parrains, Marraines, Frères, Soeurs, Bienfaiteurs, Bienfaitrices, etc., printed by Baudot (who was active from 1830 to 1848). It was these books that Troyes booksellers deployed in an attempt to cater for the completely new demands that were being articulated by three particular kinds of customer: peasants, to whom was offered a work 'in which one learns what it is essential to know' (calculation and arithmetic, surveying, pharmacopoeia, the composition of private agreements and letter-writing); servicemen, who had been shaped into a distinct community by the wars of the Revolution and Empire; children, or their teachers, by this time subjected to the ritual of New Year's greetings. But only one Troyes edition can be found for each of these titles – which suggests they had little success.

There are two considerations that might account for this. On the one hand, Troyes booksellers now had substantial rivals in the wide-circulation book market. Anner-André, the son-in-law of widow André, published (in 1834, 1835 and 1838) several editions of a *Nouveau Secrétaire Français* that was structured in much the same way as those published in Paris during the first two decades of the century. But in 1830 and 1840, Anner-André had to face competition on this same general title from seven Parisian publishers (including Moronval, the Ardant brothers and Le Bailly) and ten provincial publishers (including the Barbou brothers in Limoges, Offroy the Elder and Chaillot in Avignon, Pellerin in Épinal, and also the booksellers of Besançon, Reims, Clermont-Ferrand and Marseilles). In the same way, *Les Nouveaux Complimens* was also published by Parisian booksellers. During the first half of the nineteenth century, wide-circulation books were published in an ever-increasing number of towns and cities across France. There were many booksellers, both in Paris and in provincial towns that were not traditional chapbook centres, who printed the same titles in identical low-cost publishing formulas aimed at a 'popular' readership. And, as a result, the ancient supremacy of the Bibliothèque bleue producers was breached.

There is no doubt that the attraction of manuals like the *Nouveau Secrétaire Français* lay in their universality, for they brought together in a single work materials that were traditionally kept separate: letters of congratulation, which taught social etiquette and which accounted for most of the court society *secrétaires*;

commercial letters and forms, included in those manuals aimed specifically at merchants; models made necessary by the new forms and formalities of social life (that appear, for example, in the three titles published by the Troyes booksellers in the first half of the nineteenth century). By juxtaposing letter models that related to different new and old epistolary genres and practices, the various versions of the *Nouveau Secrétaire Francais* appealed to a broad and very diverse readership that ensured their success at least into the mid century – and even later given that the title ran to fourteen editions in the 1850s and ten in the 1860s (in the collection of the Bibliothèque Nationale alone).

At the beginning of the nineteenth century, most letter-writing manuals appeared to undergo a change of status. With the advances in written communication, which had become both more necessary and more ordinary (at least in certain popular environments), collections of specimen letters fulfilled a practical purpose which formerly they had lacked. The new letter-writers, as described by Gavarni in a series entitled 'La boîte aux lettres', published in *Le Charivari* between July 1837 and February 1839, were hesitant writers, rather unsure about spelling and clumsy in their observance of correct form. One of them, a young girl writing to her sweetheart, was still obliged to resort to the mediation of the public letter-writer. But all the others (servants, artisans, shopkeepers, cooks, milliners) were adept and more or less expert authors of the letters they wrote – to their loved ones, to their closest friends, to the Minister of Finance (addressed as 'S Ex Mons. le Ministre des finances'), to the 'members of the disciplinary committee of the First Battalion'. The most directly utilitarian manuals published in the first few decades of the century could certainly be of great help to them. It was therefore when letter models were no longer available in chapbook format that they became really 'popular', that is, employed by the majority of their purchasers in accordance with their explicit purpose. This conclusion must not, however, obscure the gap that persisted between the social world conjured up in nineteenth-century *secrétaires* and the one actually inhabited by ordinary letter-writers – a distance that left room for readings other than those governed by sheer utility. Yet it does mean that the start of the nineteenth century saw the end of the paradoxical connection forged two centuries earlier between Puget de La Serre and the Oudot or the Garnier, between a wholly aristocratic epistolary civility and a publishing venture aimed at the lowliest of readers.

Notes

Part of the information presented in this essay is derived from preliminary research undertaken by Maryvonne Pérez. I should like to thank her for her contribution.

1 A.D., Aube, 2E, Robbin minutes, Inventory of the printworks, the foundry and the printed merchandise belonging to Étienne Garnier, 28 January/21 February 1789.

2 A.D., Aube, 2E, Jolly minutes, Inventory and assessment of the merchandise of Jacques Oudot, 18 June/17 July 1722. Identification of the Troyes *secrétaires* is based on A. Morin, *Catalogue descriptif de la Bibliothèque bleue de Troyes* (*Almanachs exclus*) (Geneva: Librairie Droz, 1974).

3 The title has been thus described by A.-A. Barbier, *Dictionnaire des Ouvrages Anonymes* (Paris, 1879), vol. 4, col. 455: *Secrettaire (le) comprenant le stile et méthode d'escrire en tous genres de lettres missives (...) illustré d'exemples (...) extraits de plusieurs sçavans hommes par G.C.T. (Gabriel Chappuys Tourangeau)*, Paris, Abel L'Angelier, 1568. The attribution to 1568, reproduced in A. Cioranescu, *Bibliographie de la littérature française du XVIIe siècle* (Paris: Klincskieck, 1959), p. 198, as well as by many others, is undoubtedly mistaken. Abel L'Angelier only became a bookseller in 1572 (according to D. Pallier, *Recherches sur l'imprimerie à Paris pendant la Ligue (1585–1594)* (Geneva: Librairie Droz, 1975), p. 484).

4 G. Gueudet, 'Les premiers manuels français d'art épistolaire', in *Mélanges sur la littérature de la Renaissance à la mémoire de V.-L. Saulnier* (Geneva: Librairie Droz, 1984), pp. 87–98.

5 W. D. Patt, 'The Early "*Ars Dictaminis*" as Response to a Changing Society', *Viator. Mediaeval and Renaissance Studies* 9 (1978), pp. 133–55.

6 R. Prigent, 'Le Formulaire de Tréguier', in *Mémoires de la Société d'histoire et d'archéologie de Bretagne*, vol. 4 (1924), pp. 275–413.

7 J. Gurkin Altman, 'The Letter Book as a Literary Institution 1539–1789: Toward a Cultural History of Published Correspondences in France', *Yale French Studies* 71 (1986), pp. 17–62, and 'Pour une histoire culturelle de la lettre: l'épistolier de l'État sous l'ancien

régime', in M. Bossis and C. A. Porter (eds), *L'Épistolarité à travers les siècles. Geste de communication et/ou d'écriture*, Centre Culturel International de Cerisy-la-Salle (Stuttgart: Franz Steiner Verlag, 1990), pp. 106–15.

8 Mary Saint Francis Sullivan, *Étienne du Tronchet: auteur forézien du XVIe siècle. Étude biographique et littéraire* (Washington: Catholic University of America, 1932).

9 J. Basso, 'Les traductions en français de la littérature épistolaire italienne aux XVIe et XVIIe siècles', *Revue d'Histoire Littéraire de la France* (Nov.–Dec. 1978), pp. 906–18, and *Le Genre épistolaire en langue italienne (1583–1662). Répertoire chronologique et analytique* (Nancy: Presses Universitaires de Nancy, 1990).

10 'A Consideration upon Cicero', in *The Complete Works of Montaigne*, trans. Donald M. Frame (London: Hamish Hamilton, 1958).

11 E. R. Curtius, *European Literature and the Latin Middle Ages*, trans. William Trask (Princeton: Princeton University Press, 1973), pp. 75–6.

12 J. Hoock and P. Jeannin, *Ars Mercatoria. Handbücher und Traktate für den Gebrauch des Kaufmanns/Manuels et traités à l'usage des marchands 1470–1820. Eine analytische Bibliographie*, vol. 1: *1470–1600* (Paderborn: Ferdinand Schöning, 1989), pp. 169–71, 540–1, 960–3.

13 *Livres populaires du XVIe siècle. Répertoire sud-est de la France*, under the responsibility of G. Demerson (Paris: Éditions du CNRS, 1986), pp. 359–60, 375–6.

14 Erasmus, *De Conscribendis Epistolis*, ed. J.-C. Margolin, in *Opera Omnia Desiderii Erasmi Roterodami*, ordinis primis, tomus secundus (Amsterdam: North-Holland Publishing, 1971), pp. 153–579.

15 M. Fumaroli, 'Genèse de l'épistolographie classique: rhétorique humaniste de la lettre, de Pétrarque à Juste Lipse', *Revue d'Histoire Littéraire de la France* (Nov.–Dec. 1978), pp. 886–98.

16 J. Chupeau, 'Puget de La Serre et l'esthétique épistolaire: les avatars du "Secrétaire de la Cour" ', *Cahiers de l'Association Internationale des Études Françaises*, no. 39 (May 1987), pp. 111–26.

17 Baron Ernouf, 'Puget de La Serre. Sa vie et ses oeuvres', *Revue Contemporaine*, 2nd series, 51 (1866), pp. 681–712.

18 M. Fumaroli, *L'Age de l'éloquence. Rhétorique et 'res literaria' de la Renaissance au seuil de l'époque classique* (Geneva: Droz, 1980), pp. 542–51.

19 C. Jouhaud, 'Power and Literature: The Terms of the Exchange, 1624–1642', in *Administration of Aesthetics, Censorship, Political Criticism and the Public Sphere* (Minneapolis: University of Minnesota Press, 1994), pp. 34–82.

20 Puget de La Serre, *Le Secrétaire de la Cour ou la Maniere d'escrire selon le temps. Augmenté des Compliments de la Langue Françoise, A. M. de Malherbe, Nouvelle Edition, revue et corrigée* (Paris: Charles Silvestre, 1634), London, British Library 1578/1136.

21 B. Bray, *L'Art de la lettre amoureuse des manuels aux romans (1550–1700)* (Paris and The Hague: Mouton, 1967).

22 Puget de La Serre, 'Au lecteur', in *Le Secrétaire à la Mode ou Methode facile d'escrire selon le temps diverses Lettres de Compliment, Amoureuses et Morales* (Paris: Olivier de Varennes, 1640), London, British Library 10910 aaa 23.

23 Ibid.

24 A. Willems, *Les Elzevier. Histoire et annales typographiques* (Brussels, Paris and The Hague, 1880), pp. 246, 566, 568 and 591; *Catalogue d'une collection de volumes imprimés par les Elzevier et divers typographes hollandais du XVIIe siècle*, composed by E. Rahir (Paris, 1896), nos 963, 1012, 1029, 1041, 1129, 1208, 1328, 1961, 2057 and 2255.

25 Puget de La Serre, *Le Secrétaire à la Mode. Augmenté d'une instruction d'escrire des lettres: cy-devant non imprimée. Plus un recueil de lettres morales des plus beaux esprits de ce temps. Et des Complimens de la langue françoise* (Amsterdam: Louis Elzevier, 1644), London, British Library 10910 a 11, with a frontispiece dated 1645.

26 Puget de La Serre, *Le Secrétaire à la Mode ou Méthode facile d'escrire selon le temps diverses Lettres de Compliment, Amoureuses et Morales. Augmenté des Complimens et Elégances françoises accommodées au langage du temps, cy-devant non imprimées*, based on the copy printed in Paris, 1641, Paris, Bibliothèque Nationale, Res. Z 4106.

27 Fumaroli, 'Genèse', p. 896.

28 R. Chartier, 'From Texts to Manners. A Concept and its Books: *Civilité* between Aristocratic Distinction and Popular Appropriation', in R. Chartier, *The Cultural Uses of Print in Early Modern France*, trans. Lydia G. Cochrane (Princeton: Princeton University Press, 1987), pp. 71–109. See in particular pp. 80–2 on the *Nouveau Traité de la civilité qui se pratique en France parmi les honnêtes gens* by Antoine de Courtin, 1671.

29 'Instruction à escrire des lettres', in *Le Secrétaire à la Mode* (Amsterdam, 1644), pp. 3–50.

30 The full title of this edition is *Le Secretaire à la Mode. Augmenté d'une instruction d'escrire des lettres, cy-devant non imprimée. Avec un Recueil de Lettres morales des plus beaux esprits de ce temps. Plus les devis d'un Cavalier et d'une Demoiselle. Et de nouveaux*

Complimens de la langue Françoise, lesquels n'ont esté encore veus (Rouen: Robert Doré, 1651), Paris, Bibliothèque Nationale, Z 13 384. The *Secretaire*, the *Recueil* and the *Devis* form a single bibliographical unit resulting from a single composition, as is indicated by a comparison of the signatures (a–r 12), and the *Complimens* another unit (A–C 12). Each unit has its own pagination ([1]–407 and [1]–75), but the existence of a single table of contents (composed in D 6) indicates how frequently they were combined.

31 H.-J. Martin and M. Lecocq, with the collaboration of H. Carrier and A. Sauvy, *Livres et lecteurs à Grenoble. Les registres du libraire Nicolas (1645–1668)* (Geneva: Libraire Droz, 1977), vol. 2, pp. 589–90.

32 Puget de La Serre, *Le Secrétaire à la Mode ou Méthode facile d'écrire selon le tems diverses Lettres de Complimens, Amoureuses et morales* (Troyes: Veuve Jacques Oudot and fils Jean Oudot, 1730), A–O 8/4.

33 R. Chartier, 'Publishing Strategies and What the People Read, 1530–1660' and 'The Bibliothèque bleue and Popular Reading', in Chartier, *The Cultural Uses of Print*, pp. 145–82, 240–64 (esp. pp. 175–82, 257–63).

34 K. Gee Hornbeak, 'The Complete Letter Writer in England 1586–1800', *Smith College Studies in Modern Languages* 15, nos 3–4 (Apr.–July, 1934), esp. pp. 66–72. 'Appendix II' to this essay provides 'A Bibliography of the English Letter-Writer 1586–1800', pp. 128–45.

35 *Le Secrétaire des Dames. Pour apprendre à écrire de belles Lettres en langue française* (Troyes: Chez Garnier, permission dated 1759), A–B 8/4, Paris, Bibliothèque Nationale, Res. pZ 2169 [1–8].

36 F. Colletet, *Le Nouveau Secrétaire Français ou l'Art de bien écrire et dicter toutes sortes de Lettres sur les sujets qui arrivent dans la Société civile* (Troyes: Garnier, n.d.; permission dated 17 Oct. 1738), Troyes, Bibliothèque Municipale, Bibliothèque bleue 758. Two other editions were published under permissions granted earlier to Pierre Garnier: one on 6 May 1728 (Troyes, Louis Morin collection), the other on 17 July 1736 (Troyes, Bibliothèque Municipale, Bibliothèque bleue 149). I should like to thank Marie-Dominique Leclerc, historian of the Bibliothèque bleue, for the help she has given me in tracing this title. Although it is altogether probable that the work of François Colletet went through one or more editions prior to its mention in the catalogue of the Oudots and the Garniers, I have not yet been able to trace such an edition. It is quite certain, in any case, that *Le Nouveau Secrétaire Français* was not a simple

republication of the letters published by Colletet in *L'Académie familière des filles: Lettres, et diversitez folâtres de prose et de vers. Suite de la Muse coquette. Troisième et quatrième partie* (Paris: Jean-Baptiste Loyson, 1665), pp. 63–116.

37 E. Auerbach, *Mimesis: The Representation of Reality in Western Literature* (Princeton: Princeton University Press, 1953), pp. 285–311.

38 Puget de La Serre, *Le Secrétaire du Cabinet ou la Manière d'écrire que l'on pratique à la Cour*, 6th edn (Paris: Michel Bobin, 1680), London, British Library 1089 a 13.

39 Puget de La Serre, *Le Secrétaire de la Cour ou La Manière d'écrire selon le temps. Augmenté de Complimens de la Langue françoise. Inscription des Lettres, et la Doctrine amoureuse* (Lyons: Antoine Bresson, 1713), London, British Library, 1085 g 11.

40 I should like to thank P. Jeannin and J. Hoock for allowing me to consult their data file of titles and descriptions of manuals for the use of traders published in the eighteenth century.

41 P. Caspard, 'L'amour et la guerre. Lettres d'un soldat neuchâtelois à sa fiancée pendant la guerre de Sept Ans', *Musée Neuchâtelois* (1979), no. 2, pp. 72–91 (letters quoted on pp. 80, 82, 87).

42 P. Caspard, ' "Mon cher patron". Lettres d'un ouvrier suisse à ses employeurs (1770–1811)', *Milieux*, 3–4 (Oct. 1980), pp. 50–63 (letters quoted on pp. 58, 59).

43 R. Chartier, 'The Literature of Roguery in the Bibliothèque bleue', in Chartier, *The Cultural Uses of Print*, pp. 265–342.

44 R. Chartier, 'The Hanged Woman Miraculously Saved: An *Occasionnel*', in R. Chartier (ed.), *The Culture of Print: Power and the Uses of Print in Early Modern Europe*, trans. Lydia G. Cochrane (Cambridge: Polity, 1989), pp. 59–91.

45 *Le Nouveau Secrétaire Français ou Modèles de Lettres sur toutes sortes de sujets* (Paris: Le Prieur, 1804); it was republished by the same publisher in 1810, 1811, 1813, 1819 – the 'twelfth edition' – 1822, 1824 and 1829.

46 *Le Nouveau Secrétaire Français contenant des Modèles de Lettres de Bonne Année, de Fêtes, de Félicitation et de Condoléance, de Remerciement, d'Affaires et de Commerce, de Recommandation, etc.* (Paris: Moronval, 1827); the book was republished by the same publisher in 1830, 1832, 1837 and 1840.

47 J. Gurkin Altman, 'Teaching the "People" to Write: The Formation of a Popular Civic Identity in the French Literature', unpublished paper. I should like to thank Janet Gurkin Altman for allowing me to see this text and for her help.

3

Letter-Writing Manuals in the Nineteenth Century

Cécile Dauphin

The interest shown by the publishing industry in a particular subject can throw considerable light on social practices. The varying relative volume of religious books published helps, for example, to clarify developments in religious beliefs and devotional behaviour. The same index can be applied to politics, the life of the imagination or to specific practices such as travel, cookery and astrology. Viewed in this way, letter-writing manuals are a particularly valuable source of information for the history of ordinary writing: they can be seen as both instrument and symptom of the spread of letter-writing as well as of the growing circulation of letters during the course of the nineteenth century.

Is it possible to come up with an immediate definition of the letter-writing manual? Teaching anthology, pseudo-novel in the form of a family chronicle, mass of outmoded expressions, vestige of amorous preciosity? When dictionaries accepted that *secrétaire* should be understood in the sense of a letter-writing manual, they defined it, from the seventeenth century down to our own day, as a 'manual containing model letters for the use of people who are not at all accustomed to the art of writing'.[1] The *Larousse du XXe siècle* considered these books to be appropriate for people 'unable' to write letters by themselves. This nuance refers back on the one hand to the familiarity with the art of writing in general and, on the other hand, to the more specific ability to compose letters. But at other times, other dictionaries (the *Richelet*, the dictionary of the *Académie Française*, the *Grande Encyclopédie*, the *Robert*, the *Petit Larousse*) simply dispense with any mention of the existence of such manuals under the heading *Secrétaire*. What can be noted therefore is the continued existence of the *secrétaire* over the long term but also the hesitation of lexicographers to give the genre legitimacy by according it a place in their dictionaries.

But definitions do not exhaust content. The true status of the letter-writing manual is not apparent at a first reading. What matters therefore is to identify its place in the overall publishing output, to describe the body of letter-writing manuals published between 1830 and 1900 and then to attempt to decipher the ways in which they were used.

A publishing practice

Measurements

The *Bibliographie de la France*[2] dispenses rapidly with 'epistolary style' in its 'Belles-Lettres' section. It lumps together editions of the correspondence of Madame de Sévigné or Voltaire, love letters, *secrétaires* great, small, modern, new, universal . . . and a variety of commercial and administrative formularies. Everything, that is, that has anything to do with letter-writing.[3]

Careful selection of the available titles was vital in order to create as homogeneous a body of texts as possible. Proceeding by elimination, the literary editions of letters by writers or by historical characters presented as such were the easiest to detect and weed out. Forms intended exclusively for commerce and administration, aimed at a specific readership and having their own specific features, were also beyond the range of our research. It was less straightforward to mark out the boundaries separating letters to celebrate fêtes and compliments – verses, bouquets and *corbeilles* – designed to 'decorate the memory of the children', that ranged from flysheets to a 216-page collection in duodecimo format.[4] There was cause to hesitate before material that combined written and oral language, words and music and letters containing the most varied of verse. Some of this work, providing it featured at least a handful of model letters, was included in the survey. But most of this ample and diverse crop was excluded from this first approach.

Although no enquiry of this type can claim exhaustiveness, a process of sorting through book titles was needed to investigate a terrain that, with the exception of a very few exhumed fragments,[5] remains largely unexplored, with many uncertain and shadowy outlying areas and a very blurred perimeter. Be that as it may, the investigation brought to light 195 titles and 616 editions, stored at the Bibliothèque Nationale, covering the period from 1830 to 1899.[6] This rough-and-ready statistic demonstrates that there was considerable interest among publishers for what was after all a relatively specialist subject.[7]

To judge by certain contemporary accounts, epistolary manuals were extremely common: they were to be found 'under the washing' that the maid had to iron;[8] 'the boxes of the secondhand booksellers along the Seine were full of them';[9] and the pedlar's pack would also be well stocked with them. Reports are quite clear: 'these booklets are extremely numerous and constantly in fashion.'[10] 'The number of books that have been published on this subject is quite prodigious and surprising quantities of them are sold every day: their entire usefulness is so well recognized!'[11] Such enthusiasm should however be moderated: according to one statistic relating to books printed between 1814 and 1833,[12] epistolary manuals only accounted for 2 per cent of all belles-lettres. On average, judging by our corpus, about eight manuals were published annually between 1830 and 1899. Compared with the 10,000 or so books published in France each year, this was a mere drop in the ocean.[13]

If the selection of epistolary manuals from the *Bibliographie de la France* and the catalogues of the Bibliothèque Nationale may be taken to represent nineteenth-century output in this genre, it can serve as a useful object for chronological, geographical and publishing analyses.[14]

An initial distinction has to be made between books by named authors and anonymous works. Even if it is reasonable to assume that a great deal of slippage from one category to the other was typical of the genre (books by named authors reprinted without their signatures or the plagiarization of anonymous works by named authors) and even if many investigative leads seem to have faded beyond recall, the chronology of these two categories none the less displays several special features (see the figure). For the 1830s, only 24 manuals by named authors could be found. This figure doubled in the 1840s, then tripled and then quadrupled between 1850 and 1870. A peak of about 100 manuals was reached in the 1860s. The downturn was as swift and as steady as the increase: by the last decade of the century, our survey contains a mere 13 manuals by named authors. As for anonymous works, output appears stable between 1830 and 1860 at roughly 50 manuals per decade. The downturn, although it began somewhat earlier, ran parallel with that of signed manuals.

A comparison of these two curves suggests that named authors picked up where the lengthy succession of Bibliothèque bleue *secrétaires* left off. Anonymous publication remained the general rule until the 1840s, in keeping with almanac and chapbook tradition. The drop in output of anonymous works seems indeed to be related to the decline in book-hawking. With the blow inflicted by the press law of 27 July 1849, which subjected book-

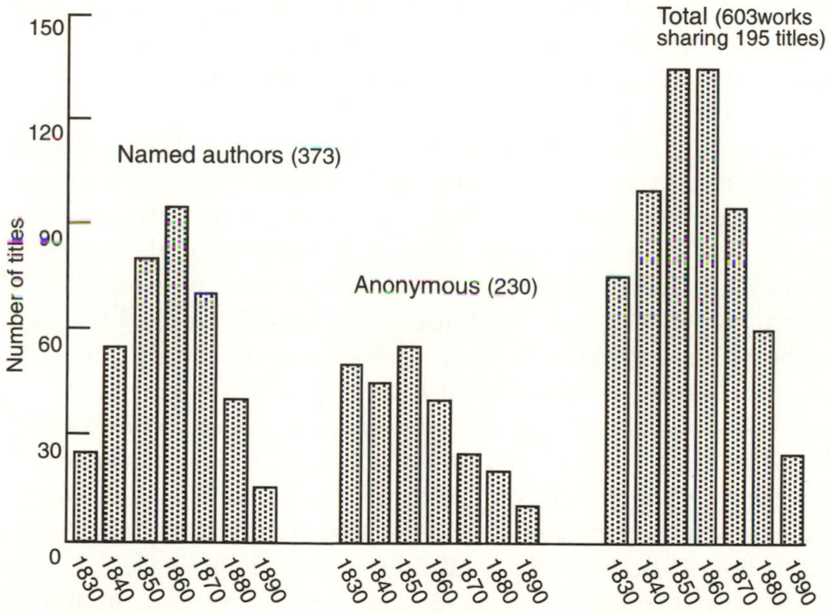

Publication of epistolary manuals, 1830–1899 (including new editions and reprints)

hawking to authorization by local police chiefs, and under the surveillance of the permanent commission on chapbooks from 1852 to 1870, book-hawkers lost their ability to trade. Books were becoming more generally traded commodities:[15] stacked on grocers' shelves 'between pepper and candles', sold from railway station bookstalls or from the new bookshops, epistolary manuals survived – but now bore their authors' names. At the same time, chapmen retreated from the market and new authors turned their hand to epistolary manuals. It was as though *secrétaires* could only secure their survival and sales by equipping themselves with a name.

But the decline of the chapbook does not explain away everything. Books by named authors became the rule prior to the Second Empire. In this blossoming-out of vocational letter-writing authors, a link can be seen with the development of publishing for schools. As we emphasize below, children were one of the main targets of letter-writing manuals. The earliest legislation on schooling presented a golden opportunity for a variety of authors (publishers, teachers and others) to draw on traditional *secrétaires*, update them, and serve them up under the guise of education. On their way to the classroom, chapbooks lost their blue covers and gained a guarantee of experience and an institutional brand of approval.

The distinction between signed and anonymous books within the output of letter-writing manuals should not obscure the overall trend: growth under the July Monarchy, a boom under the Second Empire and then a sharp downturn at the turn of the century. Whatever the output of letter-writing manuals may have been prior to 1830, it certainly did not compare with the level reached by the 1850s. The epistolary genre could trace its family tree back into the distant history of twelfth-century treatises known as *ars dictaminis* or *dictandi*, or indeed to ancient times: an unbroken thread running from Cicero down to our own day. Yet it seems that the publishing explosion of the nineteenth century eventually overexposed its numerous branches: after a period in full bloom, only a few withered limbs lived on to save the species.[16]

The output of letter-writing manuals thus followed a curve that was quite independent of general trends in publishing. Whereas the publishing industry as a whole benefited from the general economic upturn and steadily expanded throughout the nineteenth century,[17] the output of letter-writing manuals plummeted towards the end of the century, suggesting that it was a quite specific cultural phenomenon. The spread of the civilization of printed matter goes some way toward explaining the mushrooming of this kind of book at the beginning of this period but it was not vigorous enough to sustain it. Public education, involving a process of apprenticeship, rendered the manual obsolete and shrank its customer base. Its usefulness in education and the very successes of acculturation through schooling carried with them the seeds of its undoing.

Our two hypotheses, that the publication of letter-writing manuals followed its own chronological pattern and that authors seized possession of the tradition of anonymity, find support in the way that the publication of letter-writing manuals was distributed geographically. Most of the signed manuals (eight out of ten) were published in Paris. The role of the provinces was pared down to a bare minimum (one manual out of every ten). The other 10 per cent of author-written manuals bore twin Parisian and provincial addresses, or were printed abroad (Belgium, the Netherlands and Germany). Of the anonymous manuals, in contrast, many more were published in the provinces, Paris producing only six out of every ten.

Even more significant was the spread of manuals between the 'two Frances' that appear as rivals throughout the history of French publishing: north of the Loire (except for Brittany), provincial printing was more firmly established; south of this line (which diverges somewhat from the Maggiolo pattern), southern France appears comparatively underendowed in publishing enterprises.[18] Yet, of the total output of letter-writing manuals, only those compiled by named authors fit this general pattern. Most anonymous manuals, on the other hand, were produced in provincial France south of the Loire. This pattern of geographical distribution does not correspond to the overall pattern of publishing as a whole, still less to modern economic and cultural realities: once again Paris plays a preponderant role, now even more so than for publishing generally (according to Barbier, 10 per cent of books were published in Paris around 1840). Outside Paris, authors, though still not very numerous, tended to publish in the north-east, in line with the general pattern. Anonymous works, on the contrary, were mostly published in the central and southern regions.[19]

If it was often chapbook publishers that published letter-writing manuals – the names cited by Nisard in the mid-nineteenth century also figure on the covers of the manuals[20] – it is more surprising to observe their preponderance south of the Loire, bearing in mind that, again according to Nisard, most chapbook publishers were based in the towns of north-east France. One might think, in line with the hypothesis that the *secrétaire* was brought up to date with the aid, among other things, of a signature, that this renewal was first and foremost the achievement of Parisian and north-eastern publishers, quicker to adopt new technology and the latest innovations in publishing. South of the Loire, traditional practices, including anonymity, survived longer.

J.-J. Darmon has stated that there was no Parisian or provincial publisher who had not, at one time or another, helped to swell the book-hawker's pack with some book or other, whether recent or secondhand. Similarly, it seems that there was no publisher who had never given in to the temptation to compile a *secrétaire*, whether signed or unsigned: our corpus contains the names of at least 143 different publishers. On average, there was just about one title per publishing house and roughly three new editions per title. In this respect, there was little difference between manuals by named authors and anonymous works: on average the former ran to 3.2 separate editions and the latter to 2.9.

These very modest ventures met with varying success. The big names in publishing did not look askance at letter-writing manuals and, judging by the number of new editions, they certainly managed to market their own products. Between 1854 and 1900, Garnier published 10 titles, running to at least 56 editions, not counting those that continued into the twentieth century. Hachette, with 9 titles and 29 separate editions, produced letter-writing manuals designed for school use only. However, although they had the greatest number of authors, their titles went through relatively few editions. Among the other publishers who were particularly active in this field, Lebailly had 10 titles running to a total of 53 editions, Bernardin-Béchet 7 titles and 24 editions,

Table 1 Number of editions per *secrétaire* title (1830–1900)

	Paris	Provinces
Named authors	3.7	2.6
Anonymous works	2.8	1.8

and Langlumé-Peltier 28 editions of a single title. Provincial publishers never achieved successes to rival their Parisian counterparts. The only one to come close was Deckherr, at Montbéliard, which published 4 titles that totalled 29 editions. Ardant was something of a special case, drawing on both anonymous works and named authors, and publishing from both Paris and Limoges.

The output of manuals by named authors, centred on Paris, seems to have been concentrated in the hands of relatively few publishers. The output of anonymous works, on the other hand, appears scattered, fought over by a plethora of small-scale printer-booksellers. Table 1 affords a clear picture of this.

Forms and images

Anyone who handles and flicks through the letter-writing manuals housed at the Bibliothèque Nationale is bound to be struck by their cheap, casual and rushed appearance. More often than not they are printed on coarse paper. The pages are untrimmed. Worn-out type-faces have produced a very blurred text with some passages that are almost unreadable. Misprints abound. There are pages that are missing or in the wrong order, sometimes an entire section has been overlooked. In one particularly outlandish case, *Lettres de famille . . .* by Zulma Carraud, the manual was published by the highly professional Hachette publishing house, yet its first 24 pages come from another book, *Historiettes pour les jeunes enfants*. Titles too could vary: one book entitled *Nouveau Secrétaire de cabinet* on its cover (published by Lebigre in 1836) turned into a *Nouveau Secrétaire des . . . amants* on its title page.

The hastiest confections merely reproduced extracts from previous manuals and either dispensed altogether with a table of contents or confined themselves to giving a rough indication of page numbers and chapter titles. Although the preface and introduction, often considered as optional extras, were liable to vanish, author-publishers generally made an attempt to introduce a personal if not an original note at this point. But in the midst of all this typographic mediocrity, some well-produced works stood out, their pages well trimmed, clearly printed, their paper sometimes quite fine, the text nicely framed, with a ribbon to mark the pages. The page might also be carefully laid out, well structured, with new chapters beginning on fresh pages, detailed tables of contents and, in at least two cases, alphabetical indexes of subjects and proper names.

The general appearance of the letter-writing manual corpus is so disparate that its overall place and status in nineteenth-century publishing are hard to gauge. Although a far cry from high-priced books bound in decorated covers or from the kinds of works targeted at bibliophiles, letter-writing manuals could hardly be placed in the same category as popular books, even if certain *secrétaires*, more often than not anonymous and straight out of the Bibliothèque bleue, bore all the hallmarks of the chapbook. The urge to rehabilitate a genre that had been vilified by the world of letters while also making a profit in a still flourishing section of the market induced publishers and authors to aim for quality or, at least, to meet the publishing standards of the times. This effort can be seen in the clear separation of chapters, the attempt to arrange and present tables clearly, the addition of prefaces and introductions and, above all, the quest for originality in both the content and the form of the model letters selected.

One of the characteristic developments in nineteenth-century publishing was the invasion of printed text by illustrations[21] and letter-writing manuals did not escape this fashion. As is true of publishing as a whole, the 1840s were the decade when the greatest number of illustrated manuals was published. Sixty-four of the titles in our corpus, roughly a quarter, contained one or more illustrations (not including typographical decorations such as garlands or crowns of laurel). Mostly these illustrations took the form of frontispieces (36 pictures, plus 4 that folded out to form triple pages), carved on wood (there were only 5 lithographs), framed, separated from the text, sometimes reused in several later editions and even in other titles. Less often illustrations were used to decorate the binding (10 illustrations filling the back cover and 4 on the cover) or, in 8 cases, the title.

But in the loyalty that letter-writing manuals – like chapbooks, for that matter – showed towards woodcuts and in their strictly limited use of illustrations (only two were placed within the main text), they stood out clearly from the general publishing output which, at this time, was using an increasing number of illustrations in the main body of the text and combining different engraving and lay-out techniques.[22] In itself, illustration brought nothing new to the genre. The many publishing houses outside Paris (Limoges, Avignon, Epinal, Montbéliard, Lille) sustained the classical pattern of popular illustration: crudely sketched vignettes, framed and placed outside the main body of the text. The increasing number of illustrations included in letter-writing manuals in the mid-nineteenth century did nothing to relieve the archaism of the genre: it had more to do with sales strategies designed to bring them into line with current tastes.

Illustrations of letter-writing seem to have been torn between two extremes. At one extreme was a realist approach that displayed the process of writing the letter, its transportation and its receipt. At the other extreme there was greater reliance on imagination, with a suggestion of the feelings and consequences prompted by the letter: love and its tribulations brought this second set of images into sharp focus.

The first and much larger set of illustrations, 44 out of 63, helped to fix the masculine and elitist parameters of letter-writing imagery. Of 32 scenes of people writing, only 5 women are shown in a writing position and, of these 5, one rests the paper on her knees,[23] another leans back dreamily, with a pen in her hand, another flicks through a book on a stand while the pen remains in the ink-well, yet another, in the company of a fellow pupil, writes under the direction of a teacher, while the last slavishly copies from a manual. The writing materials shown are rudimentary and the setting is intimist. In all the illustrations included in our corpus, there is not a single woman who stands business-like behind a writing-desk. Instead they use a pedestal table . . . or their knees.

The typical letter-writer was a man. Seated at his writing-desk, he would be surrounded by a certain number of items: two quills, one in his hand, the other in the inkpot; various books, either in a bookcase, on the table or scattered on the floor; a mantelpiece with a mirror and a clock; an armchair and some period furniture; a window and a globe. This, give or take a detail, was the most usual way of portraying letter-writing. It conjured up the technical conditions for writing (goose quill, inkpot, table or writing-desk), its cultural context (familiarity with printed matter), its social setting (confortable and well-to-do surroundings) and an openness to the outside world (window and globe). Some rather more lowly depictions, though still masculine, erase the bourgeois setting and limit the number of accessories. The man of the world is thus metamorphosed into a clerk or a writing journalist. If, in an extreme case, he writes from prison, he still retains his cape and his sword by his side. The 'popular' letter-writer, rather less often depicted, would resort to a third person. In the army, soldiers would dictate their letters there and then to the serving letter-writer in the presence of an officer. Public letter-writers, on the other hand, would receive dictation from a woman, modestly attired in a bonnet and apron, who would support her words with gestures and be accompanied by her mother, father or husband.

This masculine portrayal of the act of writing is offset by the essentially feminine portrayal of the receipt of the letter, which is depicted only six times. This gender division in epistolary communication foreshadows that present in model letters, where the majority of letter-writers are men,[24] even though the manuals themselves are explicitly aimed at a female readership. Above all in romantic correspondence, women expected to receive love letters but were rarely able to reply without compromising themselves. This opposition between the act of writing and the receipt of the letter casts serious doubt on the adequacy of portrayals and practices. It does in any case question the dominant role of women in domestic writing that certain corpora of letters appear to attest.[25]

The few portrayals of the way in which letters were transported are revealing, illustrating a more realistic view of epistolary communication. As early as 1845, a frontispiece displays the different stages of this process, from the public letter-writer's stall (where, once again, it is a woman who dictates the letter) to the postman who at last delivers the letter, by way of the pillar box, the mail-coach, the train and the steamship. At the end of the century, the postal service is once again depicted on a book cover illustration showing people (four women and one man) queuing up at a poste restante. But the title of this particular manual, *Nouveau Secrétaire-Guide des amoureux, Encyclopédie de l'amour*, leaves no room for any doubt as to the clandestine presence of this particular clientele in the post-office.

With the exception of four illustrations of festive occasions in which children are depicted reciting little speeches, the way in which the letter was imagined was polarized by the adventure of being in love. The technique (inclusion of lithographs) and the space occupied (three pages of frontispiece and cover and title vignettes) set these illustrations apart from 'realistic' depictions and thus attempted to seduce the readers of such manuals.[26] The lovers' story is narrated in a sequence of programme scenes arranged in the form of a medallion around Cupid: the encounter, the stroll, the conversation, the declaration, the quarrel, the reconciliation, the wedding and the marriage bed. In other compositions, scenes are arranged around letters, for example with a quarrel sparked off by a deceitful letter: 'Both the hand and the letter have lied'; or rather more banal portrayals of the lover 'seeing to his correspondence in the style of the new universal *secrétaire*' and the arrival of the postman – indeed even of the 'postman of love', metamorphosed into Cupid-Mercury.

Somewhat ignoring the letter, racy illustrations depicted couples embracing and such images were doubtless as scandalous to nineteenth-century society as were the first cinema kisses a century later. Immorality was a vital part of seduction when, evidently, women made use of a letter to betray their husbands or when the woman being courted was none other than a wet-nurse neglecting her charge. The mythological allusion to Mercury teaching Cupid in the presence of Venus[27] and the symbolism of love still appeared here and there in various title vignettes and other decorations.

Portrayals of letter-writing practice finally introduced a hierarchy into the manuals that was independent of their material quality. At the austere end of the spectrum, a dearth of illustration was typical of educational manuals intended for children and those that targeted women with a discussion of *savoir-vivre*. Belonging to a more serious genre, *secrétaires* designed for everyone displayed the process of writing as essentially masculine and elitist. As for letters of courtship, images of love suggested reverie and escape.

Illustrations embodied an attempt at seduction. To attract a readership that was unfamiliar with writing and still rather unaccustomed to reading, pictures could serve as bait. They might well fail to rehabilitate the genre in the eyes of the more literate, who, on the contrary, would see pictures as further evidence of frivolity. But in the eyes of the general public, illustration helped to invest a genre that was *a priori* rebarbative with the emotional charge that clung to the representation of letter-writing.

Playing on titles

To sustain a genre as ancient as the letter-writing manual, publishers had to resort to the art of fancy packaging and this entailed not only the use of illustrations but also clever titling. Traditionally, such works were like academies of texts (writers' letters, codes of etiquette, rules of rhetoric). From 1830 onward, it appeared that their reproduction relied less on repetition than on trying to be different.[28]

Well aware that they were straying into a dense forest, some works distinguished themselves through mockery, criticism or by appealing to their specific experience to justify adding to an already oversupplied list. Yet another *secrétaire*? The novelty of a product is a vital selling point in any advertising and marketing plan. The more familiar and commonplace a product is, the more the sales pitch has to underscore its novelty. The descriptions used to preface the books inexhaustibly described them as new, modern and fashionable, in an effort to bring an object felt to belong to the ancien régime up to date with current tastes. Yet an object's roots in the past were of undeniable value and its heritage therefore had to be handled with care: the trick was to present novelty without erasing the past, to edge away from the genre without doing anything to undermine it.

The tension that emerges from an analysis of the titles and the way that these developed during the nineteenth century clearly reveals an effort to package the manuals and to find distinctive selling points. In order to redeem a much-despised genre and to rehabilitate a discredited product, evidence had to be found in society of widespread demand and of the product's universal usefulness. This is what the titles of the manuals strove to provide.

The oldest grouping of such works were those that were termed *secrétaires*. A noble term, derived from court manners, the 'secretary' conjured up the idea of mediation, of a pen-wielding intermediary who would write on someone else's behalf. Identified with an elite culture, these *cabinet* or court *secrétaires* were direct survivors of the ancien régime. Although still very numerous at the start of the nineteenth century, they disappeared completely with the advent of the monarchy. After 1830, there was a *Secrétaire de cabinet*, published by Lebigre in Paris and called 'new' (1836), another published by Pathouot in Niort in 1836 and a third published by Delarue in Paris in partnership with Castiaux in Lille and called *Le Dernier Secrétaire de cabinet* (n.d., around 1835). As for the actual *Secrétaire de la cour de France*, only one such title was published, by Moronval, in 1830, 1832 and 1838.

Another legacy of the society of the court, the *Secrétaire français* outlived the monarchy, thanks no doubt to its identification with national culture. It sold well throughout the nineteenth century and did not disappear until the 1890s (see table 2). The last edition was published in 1883. This concluded the series of the *Grand Secrétaire français à l'usage de tout le monde*, the only French *secrétaire*, thus identified, that was modernized (by Lebailly, Par-

Table 2 Number of publications of manuals entitled *Secrétaire français*

	Anonymous	Named authors
1830–1839	20	–
1840–1849	19	4
1850–1859	20	16
1860–1869	16	12
1870–1879	4	5
1880–1889	1	–
Total	80	37

is). Advertised above all as being 'new', this title was used by the majority of anonymous works and vanished along with them, despite the fact that it was also appropriated by a number of authors: two professional publishers, Passard in Paris and Ardillier in Limoges; a professor, Deplasan; and two professional letter-writers, Dunois and de Méril, whose success as authors rested entirely on these titles.

From this trunk there arose two branches that were still thriving in the first half of the nineteenth century. First, the spate of *lovers' secrétaires*, codes of loving, recipes for happiness, dispensers of advice on matters of the heart, in which Cupid fired off his arrows with Mercury's complicity. This branch grew fairly steadily until the 1890s but tended to attract accusations of immorality that cast discredit on manuals in general. The inclusion in certain of these lovers' manuals of somewhat risqué illustrations served only to corroborate such misgivings. The second branch consisted of manuals, models, collections, guides and codes. These handbooks, which gradually vanished during the second half of the century, drew their inspiration from Philipon de La Madelaine, when they did not actually plagiarize him.[29] They relied on a twofold approach: the theory was simplified and made very accessible by a brief summary on the art of letter-writing; and classical models were always included.

With the second generation of titles, recourse to qualifying adjectives either to particularize or to universalize the genre enabled letter-writing manuals to re-emerge in large numbers in the 1850s and 1860s and to survive to the end of the period. It was from this semantic family that those manuals emerged that were still being published at the beginning of the twentieth century. Educational titles certainly accounted for the bulk of these and doubtless had the largest print runs. Letter-writing manuals were ahead of school textbooks, which did not boom until after 1875.[30] As far as authors were concerned, many of them being primary school teachers, the letter-writing manual had the advantage of being an exercise in narration, a lesson on ethics, a French language lesson (dictation and grammar) and, when the model letters were taken from published writers, a reading of literature. Yet it appears that by the 1880s the letter-writing manual, narrowly defined, had been superseded by more specific educational works (narrative, dictation . . .). How to write a letter thus became one chapter among others in the teaching of the language.

The success of letter-writing manuals was also due to the diversity of the audiences targeted – children, families, women (not to mention businessmen and officials) – and the buzz-concepts advanced to appeal to this readership: practical, illustrated, perfect, pocket, nineteenth-century. When the target was not specified, a show was made of the work's universal appeal: general, for everyone, universal, the most complete . . . As early as the seventeenth century, efforts had been made to focus attention on the wide range of situations tackled by model letters. In the nineteenth century, the detail of these circumstances was still mentioned in the titles, but the greatest emphasis was that laid on the desire to reach everyone. It was if the *secrétaire* might at last manage to quit the court and the salons and find its way instead into humble cottages simply by continually stressing the desire for universality. At the very least, the attempt at popularization was clear from the book's cover.

The art of compilation

Like flies to a honeypot, amateurs of all kinds were drawn to try their hand at manuals on letter-writing. A good place to start an investigation into the origin and sociocultural background of the authors of such manuals is the information that can be gleaned from the *Bibliographie de la France*, the general catalogue of the Bibliothèque Nationale and from passing references in the manuals themselves. There emerge a number of characteristic 'types' of letter-writing manual author. (Of the hundred or so authors included in our corpus, only in fifteen cases were we unable to discover any information.)

First of all, one can divide the authors into men and women. One can then sort the eighteen women authors (about 20 per cent of the total) into aristocrats, society women and experts on *savoir-vivre* of which letter-writing skills were an essential part.

The aristocrats include the countesses of Bradi, of Boissieux, Drohojowska, of Hautpoul-Beaufort, baronesses Staffe and Arcis, and Madame de La Fère. Most of these ladies had already published manuals on etiquette and *savoir-vivre*. Others, such as Mathilde Bourdon and Countess Della Rocca, were known for their novels or, like Zulma Carraud, for their position in literary society or, like Victoire Tinayre, for the role they played in the workers' movement.[31]

Another group of women consisted of primary school teachers: Malvina Sorlin, Mlle Bochet, the Mlles Fiot and Maria Weyer all intended their books for young children. In particular, the collections of short speeches (*compliments*) were designed to spare teachers the trouble and tedium of thinking up an original bit of verse for the start of each new school year. To this group of women one can add Henriette Large because, even though her profession remains unknown to us, she targeted her treatise at educational establishments. She had also published books on etiquette and religion. There remain a few women (Mlle Degrand, Eugénie Guérin and Charlotte Softiau) whose sole publication was a letter-writing manual.

Male authors did not take advantage of social standing to produce a letter-writing manual: it was their professional know-how that gave them their authority. Seventeen, a third of the total, were teachers at secondary level or beyond, eight were primary school teachers, including one inspector and one headteacher, three were grammarians or dictionary compilers and seven were writers.

The majority of male authors therefore were language professionals, with a strong representation of teachers. One can also count six publishers who compiled letter-writing manuals, though there were probably many others whose 'production' remained anonymous. Sometimes they hid behind pseudonyms, like Blocquel-Blismon in Lille, or behind initials, like P.C. which stood for Cuisin.

Lastly, we managed to identify four members of the legal professions (three lawyers and one notary's clerk) and two priests (authors of school books). Of the twenty-eight authors whose line of work remains unknown to us, some had already published textbooks, books of entertainment, practical guides or literary and historical studies. For the rest (about twelve), the letter-writing manual was their only published work. However, far from being negligible, these books were real bestsellers in their genre and were reissued numerous times over many years. Thus: Dunois's five titles totalled at least 39 editions between 1854 and 1968; Hocquart's one title went through 48 editions between 1845 and 1911; Persan's two titles led to 24 editions between 1838 and 1869; de Méril's two titles ran to 17 editions between 1842 and 1865.

With the exception of these acknowledged successes, the letter-writing manual was not a specialist work. It was a secondary genre produced by writers who would turn their hand to anything. The teachers who wrote letter-writing manuals tended also to write textbooks. In general, the more serious-minded of the authors also took an interest in literature (poetry, anthologies, fiction) or in history (whether they were teachers, writers, booksellers or members of the legal profession); others, more attracted by lighter genres, would attempt 'gallant' literature, song-writing, games, conjuring and various other curiosities – subjects that were also tackled by the different professional groups.

This sociological sketch underscores the diversity – teachers aside – of the cultural outlook of the letter-writing manual. It can be seen as the object of purely commercial strategies, whether these involve men of letters, grammarians or bourgeois women seeking to boost their income. As with the popular novel, nobody deliberately chose the letter-writing manual as their prime interest. As Anne-Marie Thiesse remarked with regard to popular literature,

> it was the result of previous failures in the effort to conquer a place at the heart of acknowledged and valued literature. And it was above all persons who, because of their social background (middle-class or lower), their geographical origins (provincial) or their gender (women), had little chance of struggling through long years of apprenticeship to the literary scene or of keeping themselves in the market who turned their hand to writing popular novels, often after publishing a number of works of quality.[32]

Partly because of the contempt with which the literary world treated the genre and its general lack of cultural credit, the authors of letter-writing manuals found themselves adrift in a sector of publishing in which a book's healthy return on investment mattered more than its service to art. Close to mere compilation, the publisher appropriated all the rights over a work that no longer belonged to anyone. Like a 'gleaner', as one such labelled himself, the publisher claimed the right to cut and redraft as he wished that which he considered to be common property. This explains the high proportion of anonymous works within the Bibliothèque bleue tradition.

Yet this branch of publishing was not totally given over to writers who had suffered a setback. It was also at the centre of a contest between education and entertainment, the classics and the moderns, the purists and the pragmatists. Grammarians and teachers at all levels struggled to preserve the pedigree of the letter-writing manual genre by introducing it – or more accurately, by reintroducing it – into the schools. They wanted to shore up the linguistic, literary and moral guarantees of a more widespread use of letter-writing and – over and beyond books of recipe-letters – to provide the cultural tools needed for its thorough appropriation.

A bastard genre

In general publishing terms, manuals on letter-writing occupy something of a marginal position. At the edge of literature, they comprised letters by literary authors that their compilers busily edited, selected, classified and canonized. Scintillating pages written by men and women of exceptional background or talent afford the anthologies a certain literary cachet and a guarantee of quality. But the fragmentation of the letters themselves and the way that they are detached from any context threatens to leave lovers of literature distinctly unsatisfied. Equally, readers unfamiliar with the letter-writing genre would search in vain for inspiration from such works and be most unlikely to borrow their style and form. But they might well be attracted, on the other hand, by the exotic appeal of customs and uses foreign to their own way of living.

Given that letter-writing was related to rhetoric and indeed was for a long time taught as a branch of that discipline, some manuals dealt solely with matters of theory. Whether in the form of a treatise, with its litany of precepts and definitions, or that of a catechism with its question and answer routine, the primary aim of such manuals was to preserve the 'dogma'. More concerned with formalism than with practical matters, this kind of manual, though rare by the nineteenth century, was piously pillaged and served up piecemeal in introductions to most other manuals on letter-writing.

The most run-of-the-mill kind of manual took the form of a recipe book. It was carefully targeted (at children, women, families), specialized on one subject (love, compliments . . .), kept its declarations of principle to a minimum and above all provided the greatest possible choice of model letters. Aiming to be of immediate use, such manuals encouraged their readers to use them in whatever way they saw fit, either copying the model letters word for word or adapting them as subtly as they could to their own needs.

A fourth category of manuals is distinguished by a clear intention to educate. These manuals are structured less by circumstances than by the level of difficulty involved and by the teacher–pupil relationship. They can be classified according to the age group targeted and the types of exercises used (blank spaces to be filled in, preliminary exercises, narrations, actual letters). They include a part (or volume) intended for the pupil, setting the task or specifying the subject of the letter to be written, and the part (or volume) intended for the teacher, giving the correct answer and the model. Despite the effort to adapt the material to educational ends, such exercises remain clearly wedded to literary make-believe: in some cases pupils are expected to reproduce letters penned by Madame de Sévigné, by Fénelon or by Pope Clement, starting from nothing but a summary!

Lastly, some letter-writing manuals borrow the discursive form of the novel: the protagonists are identified, or at least named, and placed in a situation that requires them to correspond. A plot then unfolds through the entire manual.[33] Sometimes the epistolary form is a mere pretext for a good gossip about *savoir-vivre* and the inculcation of proper manners.[34]

Whatever title it parades, the letter-writing manual is a bastard genre: related to literary writing, to theoretical discourse, to recipe books, to school textbooks and to epistolary novels, it resembles them all, deriving both its strengths and its weaknesses from such varied kinship. The publishing success enjoyed by textbooks and practical guides gave letter-writing manuals a boost, while the decline in the popularity of chapbooks and the generally low status of this ersatz literature hastened its decline. As one of the authors of the 'literary' branch of such manuals regretfully remarked: 'this crude and popular rhapsody, surviving to our own day, this district branch of the public letter-writer's stall has for its prime author a member of the Academy, one of the wittiest fellow-members and rivals of Boileau.'[35] This disdain for the *secrétaire*[36] indicates the gulf that had opened up between the art of letter-writing (as practised by writers) and the (utilitarian and functional) practice of letter-writing. Letter-writing manuals drank from both sources.

The spirit of the letter

The illusion of oral communication

'A letter is a conversation between people who are absent from one another [. . .] To succeed at it, imagine that you are in the presence of whomever you are addressing, that they can hear the sound of your voice and that their eyes are fixed on yours.' This definition, which appears in the *Grande Encylopédie du XIXe siècle* picks up the main theme that letter-writing manuals chorus in their prefaces and introductions. This conception, related to prayer in its effort to transcend absence and in the determination to think one's way into the other person's presence, prompted a number of developments in the manuals.

The letter appeared as a transcription of oral exchange, an extension of speech. But to identify the letter with conversation and to justify it on the grounds of the absence of the addressee is a way of cancelling out or denying the cultural distancing that is entailed. It is 'to bring down' writing, to assign it a secondary role as a mere image of 'natural' speech. Perhaps one should see this reduction of the letter to an exchange of spoken words as the necessary corollary of the popularizing claim that letter-writing was accessible to everyone. Even when it was added that to write as one speaks presupposes that one speaks well, the illusion of oral communication remained a cornerstone for the majority of letter-writing manuals.

To regard the letter as the servant of conversation was simultaneously to overrate and to underrate it. Spotting this mistake, some writers rushed to trace the outer limits of transcription: 'Writing does not convey the language of the body, that colour-shading of speech.'[37] Nor could a letter translate 'that kind of cut and thrust that occurs in conversation'; instead it possessed a 'form which is exclusively its own, a particular set of features from which it derives all its charm'.[38] Insisting that there was something subtle about letter-writing, Dezobry protested against the notion that anyone could master it.[39]

What letters lost in gestural and interactive expressiveness, they made up for in autonomy and distancing. This fundamental gain achieved in the shift from speech to writing and in the spread of written culture appears not to have been remarked upon by the authors of letter-writing manuals, locked into their stereotype of the conversation. Sommer alone pointed out in 1849 that letters were more than mere methods for reconciling oneself to someone's absence.[40] Letter-writing was necessary whenever the subject of conversation was serious enough to require more formal assurances, undertakings more binding than those that could be given by mere word of mouth, on any subject of a delicate nature for which improvisation was inadequate, or for any complicated business: in a letter one could present facts in a particular order, string them together in such a way as to impel certain consequences and make those consequences more striking. This hinted at a more complex and distanced potential status for the letter: as evidence, as a document, as a step in an official process, as a way of organizing discourse or as an instrument of reflection.

Quite evidently, writing placed distance between letter-writers and their words, entailed transformations in the way that words were ordered, and it presupposed work to elaborate both feeling and self-expression.[41] Yet letter-writing manuals did not give much credit to the creativity of writing. On the contrary, it seemed that nineteenth-century society was unable to envisage the popularization of letter-writing except in terms of a reduction of its role and status to that of mere conversation. Accordingly letter-writing was presented as within everyone's reach and its formal rules were set out as if they could be dissociated from the civilized act that was entailed. Issuing from seventeenth-century salons, conversation and letter-writing were two forms of 'commerce' that were rooted in honesty and civility. The epistolary genre (both letters and manuals), like conversation itself, was the expression of a society to which it returned its own reflection. This relatedness, which could no longer find expression except as nostalgia for a lost world and previous practices, was resistant to the popularizing drive: if epistolary art was above all the sign, the mark of a 'certain' level of education, of a familiarity with the literary canon, of a steeping in good models, how could it be reduced to a string of formulas? How could it possibly be brought out of the salons and used to cover ordinary situations and the events of everyday life? It was this fundamental ambiguity that drove the spiralling quest for situations to which to attach new models.

The impossible model

The image of the letter was not merely that of spoken words that had been written down and then conveyed across time and space. It was also to be glimpsed in the search for relevant circumstances and lived experiences. It was made plain in the titles themselves and in the lists with their claims to universality. Attempting to cover the wealth of situations that might prompt a letter, authors strove hard to include as many of them as possible and to classify them. The longer the list, the more specific and specialized it became and the harder it was for anyone to put it to use. Just to make sense of the list demanded prior experience and skill. Moreover, the kind of encyclopaedic table that resulted provided a skewed image of everyday life. The most commonplace letter (to say thank you) and the most exceptional (to petition the highest authority to pardon one's husband or son after they have been sentenced to death) were placed within a single classificatory grid that reconstructed social and affective life around fictional and normative situations.

Titles most often took the form of a systematic list of circumstances, and models too were classified in this way – especially in anonymous manuals. The process of accumulation consisted less in a search for possible situations than in the repetition of the same content in parallel forms. New Year, *fêtes*, condolences, compliments, recommendations, congratulations, thank-yous, declarations of love, announcements of weddings, births and deaths; business, commerce, bills and securities, commitments, bonds, private contracts; petitions to the king, to princes, to ministers, to officials; soldiers' letters – all of these written communications revolved around the family, love or business. Certain manuals specialized in one area, others covered the whole ground but in an order that varied. Such work entailed a process of selection and rejection in accordance with moral or educational criteria and presupposed a particular representation of social life. But, in the end, it resulted in a reduction of reality to a set of stereotyped relations.

When authors did not provide a list of circumstances in their titles, they would limit themselves to asserting the exhaustiveness of their books by using adjectives like 'great', 'general', 'the most complete' or 'universal'. It was as if all possible circumstances, cases, genres and situations were placed on display simply by making promises. Robert was not worried by any redundancy in the title he gave his book: *Grand et Nouveau Secrétaire général et universel, ou Véritable Secrétaire des secrétaires, formant le recueil le plus complet de nouveaux modèles de lettres en tous genres!*[42]

Another sort of title-cum-claim sought to convey a sense of profusion through quantification: 100 models (Lambert), 125 (Ferté), 150 (Lambert), 200 (Duménil), 340 (Neckers), and even 1,000 (Dezobry).[43] Like the piling up of adjectives, this statistical device exerted a seductive effect on the potential customer. The selling point was no longer the variety or the specificity of the situations that might plausibly prompt one to pen a letter, but rather their sheer number. This number inflation placed letter-writing firmly alongside other run-of-the-mill goods. What gained ground above all was the idea that everyday life could be dissected and divided out and its tiniest particle subjected to norms, rules and formulas.

The meticulous presentation of such a work as the *Dictionnaire pratique [. . .] avec [. . .] plus de mille modèles choisis dans les monuments et les documents de la langue française* was an extreme case of an annotated anthology of the letter-writing manual. But just as dictionary definitions do not constitute a language's syntax, so Dezobry's 'manual' failed to provide a key to letter-writing. His dictionary, like the numerous anthologies that were actually presented as such (treasury, choice of letters . . .), and the majority of manuals that mixed classical letters with specimens of their own devising, revealed the tension that underlies the whole genre, stretched between the concept of a 'work' that was constructed, published and delivered for public consumption and a 'letter', regarded as a tool of individual communication, at once specific and informal. The search for letter-triggering circumstances revealed what was at stake: the authenticity (or the truth effect) of the letters, an authenticity in terms of facts and feelings, along with and in spite of the mirages that writing entailed. It is reasonable to wonder whether the emphasis placed on circumstances and their classification did not, in the end, work to the detriment of this much-coveted authenticity.

Without making a really clean break from the traditional line of *secrétaires*, nineteenth-century manuals did, none the less, assert their interest in straightforward, ordinary, everyday life. Although society correspondence (Baroness d'Arcis) and correspondence between people of the world (Madame de La Fère) retained some emulators, ordinary circumstances (yet more frequent in signed manuals than in anonymous ones) were now presented as the central concern. But what is striking, once again, is the way in which the impulse to represent everday life was contradicted by the paradoxical picture that was then given of it.

Among these ordinary circumstances, *fêtes*, and the inevitable New Year, held pride of place. The model letters and words of advice that accompanied these occasions reveal a society in which the *fête* was regulated, established as a duty and translated into formulas. In the run-up to *fêtes*, children provided the main target for this promotion of writing (there were manuals that dealt exclusively with compliments and letters of best wishes composed by children). This kind of letter gave rise to the most strictly codified and most antiquated kind of expression, as if the innocence of children (relying on the traditional conception of soft plaster on which the teacher had to print good sentiments) should compensate in some way for the formalism of the procedures that were imposed. 'Wishes of happiness [. . .], here is the eternal circle in which the New Year letters are enclosed.'[44] For subject matter that even the authors of letter-writing manuals recognized as threadbare, various approaches were recommended: 'freshen up the subject by linking the expression of one's best wishes to some special circumstance', 'avoid blandness through brevity', 'give voice to your heart', and so on. If necessary, children might give their own personal note to the verse learnt by rote and copied out, with a flower or something that they penned themselves. In reality, the models available did not honour the 'good' intentions and rarely lighted upon felicitous expressions. Thus: 'What! I have a little sister! So much the better! Since you now have two children, you shall be loved all the more.' This childish exclamation on the announcement of a birth might convey the illusion of spontaneity. But too often plundered and recopied, it rang false. In the New Year greetings section, there were many illustrations of this supposed simplicity and how it could spill over into bombast. For example:

> The Creator, by making time fly and bringing round a new year, recalls to me naturally the one who down here on earth is for me a visible image of His beneficence and offers me at last the opportunity to express openly the wishes that I have formed each day in the secrecy of my heart . . .

Banality cannot serve as the basis for a model; the small events that weave the fabric of everyday life are ill-suited to moral edification and quite unable to fire the imagination. The letters of Madame de Sévigné, with their ability to discourse artfully on the 'little nothings' of life, are the obligatory and most frequently employed reference. Yet in the manuals, the imitation of this 'twittering that flitters over nothings' becomes an excuse to expound on the most varied and frequently even outlandish of subjects, far closer to fantasy than to everyday life. In this connection one might cite, for example, the 'Letter on an accident that happened to you while declaiming the account of the death of Hippolytus, at the sight of a rough sea' (Deiglun)[45] the 'Letter on a goldfinch's nest', the 'Letter on silkworms', the 'Portrait of a greedy woman' (Abrant)[46] and the 'Letter on a violent fire in a town at war' (Roussenq).[47] But did ordinary people really take up their pens to hold forth on natural disaster, greengages, the art of happily married life or the unreliability of human justice?

Recourse to the pseudo-epistolary novel in order to escape from classification according to situations and to create an effect of reality allowed authors not only to be more specific about circumstances liable to occasion the writing of a letter and to pinpoint the social position of those involved, but above all to place letter-writing within a stream of individual stories.

Epistolary time

The classification of circumstances, whatever form it takes, proceeds within the context of a general outline relating to time. The accumulation of models provides a broad image of everyday life; letter-writing exteriorizes, crystallizes and accentuates the discontinuity of oral communication by granting it a spatial and temporal dimension that makes it possible to submit it to a variety of operations. But written communication also creates its own ritual within a codified temporal framework.

First of all, correspondence by letter is punctuated by periods waiting for an answer. 'Every letter merits a reply,' the compilers of manuals enjoined unanimously. This obligation, based on the code of politeness, in fact represented a relationship to time that was quite specific to letter-writing. Unlike oral communication, written correspondence can be interrupted at any moment. It is in any case deferred for as long as it takes to deliver first the letter and then its reply. This period of suspended time, a source of both pleasure and anxiety, was also subject to codification in the manuals. Those *secrétaires* that were targeted at lovers, in particular, made great and complex play of time spent waiting for an answer, the faked rush to reply or the mysterious silence . . .

The time relation was also expressed in the unfolding of the annual cycle with its recurrent high points (New Year, birthdays, patronal festivals, etc.) and with its empty moments that letters had to fill. The life cycle itself also accounted for a considerable amount of correspondence, following births, marriages and deaths, with the obligatory discourses on happiness and unhappiness. This cyclical time was itself punctuated by events of symbolic importance such as military service (departure, return, the fiancée's wait), placing a child out to nurse (search for addresses, the stages of the child's growth, its homecoming or death), education (arrival at school, *fêtes*, moral and religious duties). Lastly, the rural mode of life (that of the rentier landowner), which formed the traditional and stereotypical background to numerous models, likewise imposed its particular rhythm (harvesting, grape-picking, the seasonal commuting of the bourgeois between town and country).

Letter-writing time, as represented in the manuals, determines a number of different intermeshing cycles that structure both social and emotional life. Above all, it implies an amount of free time without which written communication would be difficult. To carry on a correspondence presupposes that one has several hours a day to devote to it. Yet this relation with time, a vestige of aristocratic conceptions of social life which remained profoundly embedded in the spirit of nineteenth-century letter-writing, received a severe jolt from a 'modern' current that attached value to productive work, individual qualities, and merit as opposed to birth. The increasing amount of space given over in the manuals to concerns regarding efficiency in professional and administrative relations (tips on how to write out the address, franking, business letter style and book-keeping) provides a corrective to this image of time frittered away in idleness.

The social order

Obviously, given their normative purpose, letter-writing manuals reflected back at society the precise image that society wished to project while reinforcing the kinds of rules and social order that were worthy of conservation. But in the tangle of their outdated legacy – in which, as in the case of folk tales, interpolations and variants could no longer be distinguished – they gave the impression of being neither quite the same nor entirely different. What they reproduced therefore was a model of a society that was highly hierarchical, almost sclerotic, despite the principles of universality and the spread of culture that they also conveyed.

Nobody could depart from the law that obliged one to know and to stick to one's place on the social ladder. Age, gender, rank and power were the four unavoidable parameters. There was nothing particularly new in this, as compared with seventeenth-century treatises on civility: every form of social life obliged individuals to evaluate and interiorize their own positions within the various hierarchies. But in letter-writing, the lack of familiarity with writing compounded the effect of distance. The letter object and the ceremonial made the barriers and the positions of superiority, inferiority or equality both concrete and visible. To achieve this inscription of hierarchies in the letter form, an apprenticeship including exercises and precepts was necessary. Developments in matters of ceremonial and the proprieties were aimed first and foremost at 'that class of persons whose education has been neglected', 'those young people who do not yet have the custom of the world', those country people more socialized to labouring on the land than to true manners, and above all women who 'to whatever rank in society they belong, always have and always will have letters to write'.

To feel clearly who one was and to whom one was speaking, never to lose sight of social condition, since equality existed only in law: these were the unbending rules inscribed in all letter-writing manuals. In a shifting society of alternating empires, monarchies and republics, the rules of social distancing were inviolable. At most one could register the cautious wish that ceremonial might be simplified. But regret was also expressed for the disappearance of the good old ways. Following the example set by works on *savoir-vivre*, letter-writing manuals functioned more as conservatories for ancient practices than as incitements to change.

Social distance was not only championed as a basic principle, it was also inscribed in model letters involving the participation of different protagonists. Most manuals retained their aristocratic character, either through the reproduction of literary models mostly derived from refined politesse and court customs, or by the fact that the letter-writers identified in the models belonged to the social elite.

These fictional characters issued of course from the pens of baronesses and countesses. But numerous authors, even though they claimed they were addressing the greatest number possible, still produced bourgeois representations of the mode of living and of social relations. Abbot Delbos, for example, in his course on epistolary style, recounted the correspondence of a schoolboy, Edouard de Saint-Martin, as he travelled around Europe.[48] Or the school-teacher Deiglun who, for the purpose of training primary school pupils, chose letter-writers from comfortable backgrounds, with two homes, one in town and the other in the country, who wrote more of 'business' than of work. Zulma Carraud conjured up the social rise and brilliant career of a merchant-tanner.

Being in possession of one's 'country', having servants who were 'attached to one's person', selecting one's furniture and cashmere from India, managing the estate, performing all kinds of civility: these were theatricalities designed to display the ways of living, leisure activities and values of, essentially, the aristocracy and the bourgeoisie. As for the audience, such social theatre staged the imperturbable play of power and allegiance: the masters dictated, commanded, ordered and orchestrated an auditorium that was submissive, consenting, even delighted 'to serve such a kind master'. All in all, 'being in service is not as disagreeable as one might imagine,' wrote a cook. 'When one gains the love of one's masters and has their trust, nothing is sweeter than to obey them' (Prudhomme).[49] There is thus a particular view of society that runs like a watermark through the model letter form. Addressed more often than not to a mass audience, the rules of hierarchy are smugly rehearsed. Yet at the same time the idealized letter, given the distance it put between life as it was lived and the theatrical show that it produced, was also an invitation to dream. This photo-love-story quality accounts at least in part for the long-running success of the genre.

Some manuals made an effort to get closer to the social milieux that they were addressing, essentially by introducing a few stock characters who would then crop up here and there. The characters that were supposed to represent the working classes comprised wet-nurses and servants, farmers and wine-growers, apprentices and workmen, not to mention rough-hewn soldiers lifted straight from the pages of some Napoleonic epic. The letters tirelessly retailed the same stereotypes: wet-nurses were neglectful, servants attentive, peasants whining and self-interested, labourers hard-working and honest, soldiers penniless, amorous and debauched. The tone and style of the specimen letters also began to shift. Without, however, studding the text with the kind of spelling mistakes that in practice were tolerated, sentences grew shorter, metaphors based on the natural world blossomed and expressions were simplified. When addressing the son of a simple labourer, the advice was that the letter 'must be written in an extremely simple style and with that slight tendency, characteristic of soldiers, to treat things light-heartedly'. And this is how a farmer in love couches his declaration: 'I am no more at my ease than if I were being tumbled in a bundle of briars. It was more than six months ago that your eyes gave me a sunburn that dries me out like heat dries those great thistles that I cut in our corn [. . .]. I have something in my chest that leaps like sheep when they hear the storm [. . .]. I will love you like good bread . . .'[50]

Lending one's quill to the working classes was thus to lend them feelings and forms of expression. Above all it was to lend them a mirror in which they were expected to recognize themselves.

Whatever evidence there is of a development in the social identity of fictional letter-writers, the stock characters appear gradually to fade, leaving behind an undifferentiated generality. A cook, laundress, seamstress, servant and wet-nurse all vanish from Prudhomme's manuals between two editions both published in the 1840s. Elsewhere, new characters were making their entrance: an orphan photographer and a novelty seller's shop assistant were chosen as model protagonists for letter-writing exercises.[51] During the course of the century, the characters that the manuals brought forward increasingly lost their social markings to compose a petty bourgeoisie more concerned with efficiency than with social distinctions.

Markings

Letters, in their purely material aspect, conveyed all the signs of recognizable social status. The franking, the envelope, the paper, the signature and the margins all served to mark out the correspondents in social terms. There were few manuals that did not devote most of their introduction to this symbolic language of social distinction.

To set the scene, the Countess of Bradi supplied in 1840 a detailed inventory of 'the writer's kit': rosewood stationery, ivory or mother-of-pearl paper-folder, a seal of fine engraved stone, a porcelain pen-holder, not to mention the many other objects that covered the writing-desk. The surroundings and the quality of the materials on display immediately situated the letter-writer in a particularly opulent interior.[52] This inventory also sketched the idea of a workplace that blends into the private domain.

At the summits of politesse and social distinction, letters would be delivered to one's home by a servant. Distrust for the postal service remained deep-rooted throughout the nineteenth century: there was a fear of indiscretions and indelicacies – especially if letters were badly folded. This provided authors with a justification for enlarging on the correct folding of letters and, no doubt, for the inclusion of a cartoon entitled 'Curiosity and indiscretion' showing two servants attempting to decipher a letter by peeping through its folds. Glue-stuck envelopes gradually replaced those constructed by the writer and closed with a seal, but they were no proof against all attempts. The new envelopes only found their way into private use via commercial and business correspondence.

The embarrassed advice that authors gave on franking reveals the hazards of administrative innovation (the generalized use of the postage stamp) and the resistance that it aroused. When geographical distance made it unavoidable, the postal service was the only way. But it was felt wise, as a precaution, to impose a tax on letters: the cost was paid by the addressee. In this way, it was thought, a public service was more likely to deliver letters intact and so recover its money. In manuals on letter-writing, resistance to franking was translated into arguments about etiquette. 'One never stamps letters addressed to persons of distinction, except when one is asking a service of them, and one must therefore have one's letters delivered by a means other than the post, for it would be most unseemly to burden them with the letter's delivery cost.'[53]

After the postal reform (1849), the boundaries of politesse shifted: 'It used to be rather impolite to frank a letter. But now, with the postage stamp, it is very impolite not to frank.'[54] But after 1870, Prudhomme was still arguing that 'franking among relatives and friends, though not impolite, would not really be appropriate: it might suggest a coldness in the relationship. Whereas, for an official, the failure to frank would border on impoliteness and might mean that the letter would not be collected from the post.' 'However,' he went on, 'for bailiffs, notaries, solicitors [. . .], stamps are not needed because delivery costs are included in the fees.' Bureaucracy thus introduced its smidgeon of equality by undermining the signs of social distinction.

With the variations possible in its format, quality, colour and decorations, paper too could act as a support for social markings. 'The use of very rough paper can only be permitted to people of the lowest class.'[55] Perfumed paper was pretentious and vulgar, coloured paper in poor taste. All the decorations introduced by fashion were to be rejected as impoliteness, barely to be tolerated in children, or relegated to the 'whims of the ladies'. The same author commented that 'only witty cooks and amorous infantrymen make use of decorated paper.' To infringe these norms was to invite ridicule. In 1847 Dufayel illustrated this situation with Noun's letter in *Indiana*, a novel by George Sand: 'And yet this chambermaid had taken the silk-finish paper and the perfumed wax from Madame Delmare's writing-desk, with style in her heart.'[56] But the right materials were not enough to give the letter the seal of distinction: it was stuffed with spelling mistakes.[57]

Social difference could be read in the blank margins, in the space left between the heading and the body of the letter, or between the body and the subscription and signature. The higher that the addressee was placed, the greater the amount of space that had to be left between the closing expression and the signature. Similarly, the repetition of the addressee's titles at each new paragraph and on the envelope emphasized the extent and majesty of the presentation. But practical considerations collided with such norms, especially when fashion and business became involved: 'De luxe stationery has enjoyed such a boom in our times,' exclaimed Bescherelle. By the end of the century, it had to be admitted, however belatedly, that 'nowadays, one covers distances so easily that one might think they no longer exist.'[58]

The hidden work of naturalness

The rules of the social game, tirelessly reproduced in the letter-writing manuals, did at least play a role in rendering different figures recognizable. It was not only compliance with the norms that enabled the members of different groups to recognize one another and to distinguish themselves from others, it was also their minor or major departures from stereotype. The ultimate distinction consisted in mastering the art of breaking the rules. This *nec plus ultra*, to which every manual referred, was called 'naturalness'. There was an abundance of definitions, everyone adding their own variant, some on 'the *negligé* of a pretty woman', others on 'the mask of the spirit', still others on 'that air of freedom and that casual step [. . .], that lively tone that makes even the slightest of trifles so interesting'. All would chorus the same refrain of 'soft ease, that kind of abandonment of thought [. . .], that style that was light but not skipping, rapid but never abrupt, nimble but not disjointed . . .'

The motif of naturalness was at the heart of the letter-writing craft, which was the very model of a literary anti-genre and it challenged *a priori* rules. It stood at the crossroads of widely differing and contradictory traditions (literary correspondence, epistolary novels and *secrétaires*), at the very point where paradoxically an attempt at naturalness and a practical formalism, art and utilitarianism, fiction and authenticity all converged.

But reduced to a brief and stereotyped examination, the leitmotif of naturalness occupied a paradoxical position in the code of proprieties. It could not signal distinction unless work was undertaken on the self and this required a psychological predisposition of a kind that could not be learnt in school. Children, women and country people, always represented as being close to nature, simplicity and spontaneity, were thus the favourite target audience of letter-writing manuals. Their supposed proximity to nature, however, did not dispense them from the need to learn naturalness. It was all the more necessary for women, in particular, to learn precisely because they were supposed to be more gifted owing to 'that flexibility of their organization and that softness in which they are raised, that makes them more suited to feeling than to thinking' (Philipon de La Madelaine, 1804 to 1871).[59]

'The first care of art must be to hide itself' (Sommer). Even if for some people this work was particularly hard, it was essential not to show it. In reality, despite the plan to popularize the art of letter-writing, the real apprenticeship took place in the school . . . of the world. One can only learn how to write through the conversation of distinguished people and the study of good models.

Later in the century, confronted with this elitist position, there emerged a conception of how writing might spread that was more rooted in culture. To learn how to write, one first had to read. The appropriation of written culture was now considered a necessary staging post on the way to letter-writing, more useful than theories and codes of propriety: 'to read is to choose and then to gather up. To choose the beautiful and good elements that one encounters in the thoughts of an author and to appropriate them for oneself, taking them into oneself through memory and reflection', letting one's reading 'infiltrate softly and slowly' (Large). The maturing of taste and judgement could not be achieved from books of recipes. The concept that familiarity with written culture might serve as an introduction to the practice of letter-writing, however, was still far from replacing the former eminently elitist representation of epistolary art.

Possession, reading, usage

Letter-writing manuals, heirs to ancien régime society, bloomed and blossomed in the nineteenth century. Through a careful choice of authors, titles, content structure and illustrations, publishers strove to modernize the genre and to broaden its readership. Its resurgence is explained as much by the hybrid status of such manuals (part anthology, part recipe book; part code of civility, part school textbook) as by the depth of their roots in a specific sociocultural context: the elimination of illiteracy in France and the development of written communication.

Letter-writing manuals were part of a drive to spread writing, even though, paradoxically, they contributed little to that end. This tension between the will to popularize and the fear of losing status was expressed through motifs of conversation, universality, naturalness and social representation.

Like mirrors, letter-writing manuals reflected the codes of a particular social circle and the way it viewed the outside world. Being illusory, they leant themselves to copying and mimicry. But even if the borrowing of codes could mask appearances, the protagonists remained none the less in their place in the social fabric.

On completing this tour of letter-writing manuals, we are faced once again with the initial question regarding actual practice. It is unthinkable that this publishing genre could have flourished and lasted so long without considerable demand. It is of course possible that the initial prompting came from publishers or educationalists eager to promote the spread of writing. But to attract so many emulators, such manuals must have found a readership. The evidence provided by the books' format, print run, pricing and distribution suggests that they were aimed at a broad audience and that they circulated widely.[60]

However, just as recipe books do not reveal much about the everyday diet of the French, letter-writing manuals do not disclose the content of the real letters that were actually penned. Ownership of a particular book never constitutes evidence about reading, still less, as in the case of *secrétaires*, about writing. In the absence of any research into the usage and utility of such books, one has to make do with a number of clues.

The manuals presented themselves as undemanding and user friendly. Durand and Meslins[61] stressed their utilitarian, functional and mediated usage:

> The villager and the near-ignorant will now no longer have any need to resort to the always doubtful and often clumsy and

> laughable ministry of the public letter-writer. He can read, or even have read to him, the chapter contents, the titles of the model letters; a child will not have any trouble copying out for him the letter that he wishes to send to his father, son, fiancée or friend; or his application to the head of the state or to some official or other . . .

The use to which the manual was put and the business of letter-writing sketched here suggest something that was rare, laborious and submitted to the mediation of the 'newly' literate, the child.

For someone who knew how to read and, however clumsily, how to hold a pen, 'having the letter he needs before his eyes, he has only to copy it, adding for himself some [. . .] details [. . .] of good sense.'[62] Complete literacy opened up a margin of choice that made it possible to borrow and appropriate some snippets from the model letters, to arrange them differently, to add one's own personal note and so, bit by bit, to cover up the reference made to the manual. All authors were quick to recommend 'plundering' but, given that the manuals aspired to a certain universality, they were aware of the risk that any overservile copier would run if his correspondent happened to own the same book of model letters.

Amorous correspondence certainly seems to have been the most exposed to this danger since to express intimate feelings demanded a stamp of authenticity that ruled out any borrowing from a model, unless the copying were very well disguised. The use of letter-writing manuals thus displays all the ambiguity of a hidden, unconfessable act which in the end was deleted from correspondence. Resorting to a model letter was part of the art of make-up.

Cases of revealing clumsiness, occasions when a writer was caught, as it were, red-handed, have still to be examined. For example, in an exchange of letters between a couple in the mid-nineteenth century, the first letter from the fiancé bore the following postscript: 'I never copy out a letter, so you must not take fright at my manner of writing' (February 1847).[63] If the lover in question felt the need to set himself apart in this way, it was because the practice of copying from models seemed to him to be very common, whereas he opted to express himself freely, whatever imperfections might result, rather than use imposed turns of phrase. There is a second reference to letter-writing manuals when a husband, owning up to a love affair, mentions as a mitigating circumstance a letter in which his mistress had egged him on, he said, 'with sentences burning with love and smoking with jealousy [. . .]. The flattering but banal terms with which she overwhelmed me must have been copied from a *Secrétaire de lettres d'amour*!' By ridiculing his lover, the husband hoped to free himself of blame: the letter-writing manual was unmasked and the feelings faded away. The authenticity of the facts mattered less than the implications that could be inferred from the poor use of a letter-writing manual, and the husband took advantage of these implications. Only mistakes in the way that manuals were used are documented. The ruse of the unfaithful husband reveals a great deal about the discredited status of letter-writing manuals in nineteenth-century society. It also gives a measure of their limited benefits to a potential user: it was not so easy to copy when one had to adopt modes of expression and a language that were foreign to one's own culture.

Perhaps, as Aragon wrote, the letter-writing manual really is nothing but 'a bizarre item of lost property whose use no one can tell'. And perhaps it is on account of their state of wear and their insignificance that letter-writing manuals have been ignored by histories of the book as well as by library inventories. Indeed, if they had not been registered for copyright at the Bibliothèque Nationale, what would we know of them today? Unsuited to the needs and living conditions of working people, they could be best classified as belonging to that limited and symbolic collection of books that every home had to have. They seemed equally useless to society's elite and to the literate world, of whose mannerisms and manias they reflected an often laughable image. In the end it was the petty bourgeoisie, eager to raise itself in the hierarchy of appearances and proprieties, that was best able to put such manuals to profitable use.

By way of conclusion, let us hear two contradictory points of view on letter-writing in the nineteenth century, both containing some truth. For the Countess of Bradi,[64] it was 'one of the scourges of our civilization, this custom of maintaining relations with people who cannot interest us in any respect whatever'. Above all, it was women who were accused by the Countess of this taste for writing during a century in which they 'held pens as often as needles'. 'The number of people furiously writing away is quite considerable, increases every day, all the more since this modern mania has not yet been registered.' But if the Countess's view was sound, it seemed that she was familiar only with her own microcosm.

Zulma Carraud, who was more rural in outlook, deplored the rarity of letters in the Berry region: 'In spite of the advances in popular education, in spite of the reduction in the tax on letters and the swiftness of correspondence, the delights of epistolary intercourse remain the privilege of the few.' With remarkable lucidity, this verdict gave precise corroboration to the findings of the postal investigation of 1847.

Notes

1 See Furetière, *Dictionnaire universel* (1690), where compliments are appended to the letters; also Littré, *Dictionnaire de la langue française* (Paris: Hachette, 1863–9); Henri Bescherelle, *Dictionnaire classique de la langue française* (Paris: Bloud et Barral, 1880).

2 For the years 1830 to 1839, I have studied in detail the *Bibliographie de la France* (Paris: Éditions Pillet), first series, 45 vols, 1810–56; and *La Littérature française contemporaine, 1827–1849*, following upon *La France littéraire* (which includes alphabetic author indexes). For the years 1840 to 1899, I used the *Catalogue général de la librairie française*, 34 vols (Paris, 1867–1945).

3 The tables of the *Catalogue général de la librairie française* from 1840 onward (vols 7 and 8), when compared with the 'authors' indexes, make it possible to identify a large corpus of letter-writing manuals. Then, after consulting the 'Authors' and 'Anonymous' catalogues of the Bibliothèque Nationale, it was possible to complete this bibliography by tracing republications, other books written by the same authors and, among the anonymous works, the proliferation of very similar and in some cases identical titles. Curiously, the 'subject' index yielded only a dozen or so titles, under the heading 'épistolaire'.

4 Eugénie and Laure Fiot, *Lettres nouvelles . . .* (Paris: P. Dupont, 1863).

5 See J.-L. Vissière, 'Prête-moi ta plume . . .: les manuels de correspondance', in *La Correspondance: édition, fonctions, signification* (Aix en Provence: Centre Aixois de Recherches Italiennes, 1984).

Also V. Kapp, 'L'art épistolaire dans les manuels scolaires du XIXe siècle', in M. Bossis and C.A. Porter (eds), *L'Épistolarité à travers les siècles. Geste de communication et/ou d'écriture* (Stuttgart: Franz Steiner Verlag, 1990), pp. 116–26.

6 We took 1830 as our starting point, since the end of the Restoration marks a major watershed in the history of French publishing. At the other end of the period, there seemed no escaping the fateful century-boundary of 1899.

7 This corpus of books published over a seventy-year period seems quite large when compared to the corpus of cookery books traced by J.-L. Flandrin: 239 works, running to 962 editions, over a period of roughly four centuries (1480 to 1890).

8 Edmond et Jules de Goncourt, *Journal*, October 1858 (Paris: G. Charpentier et E. Fasquelle, 1887–96).

9 *La Grande Encyclopédie du XIXe siècle.*

10 Charles Nisard, *Histoire des livres populaires*, 2nd edn (Paris: E. Dentu, 1864), ch. 11 devoted to 'epistoliers'.

11 This remark was repeated in various manuals including those by Person de Teyssèdre, see *Le Courrier des amants* (Paris: Lebailly, 1838), and by Louis-François Raban (pseud. of the Comte de Barins), *Le Parfait Secrétaire général* . . . (Paris: Lebailly, 1849).

12 H. Bancelin-Dutertre, *Annuaire des imprimeurs*, 5 vols (Paris, 1828–45).

13 For an overall view of book publishing in France, see R. Chartier and H.-J. Martin (eds), *Histoire de l'édition française*, vol. 3: *Le temps des éditeurs. Du romantisme à la Belle Epoque* (Paris: Promodis, 1985; Fayard, 1991) (this monument of historiography, however, devotes only seven lines to *secrétaires*). See, in particular, the entry by F. Barbier, 'Une production multipliée', pp. 103–21. See also D. Bellos, 'Le marché du livre à l'époque romantique: recherches et problèmes', *Revue Française d'Histoire du Livre*, no. 20 (1978), pp. 647–60.

14 The figures given here provide an overall indication of the volume of production but are not always precise to the nearest few books. In the case of anonymous works, I counted one title per catalogue card stored in the Bibliothèque Nationale. But the precise copy of a particular manual is sometimes allocated its own separate card. Conversely, a series of reprintings entered on a single card does not rule out even quite substantial changes in content. There is no doubt that the Bibliothèque Nationale does not possess every single printing of every single work and that foreign counterfeits also slipped through its net. Yet only a fraction (about 30 titles) of the manuals

registered in the *Bibliographie de la France* are not stored in the said library. Most of these were foreign editions (Berlin, Breslau, Leipzig, Zutphen, Vienna, Liège and Roulers).

15 J.-J. Darmon, *Le Colportage de librairie en France sous le Second Empire, grands colporteurs et culture populaire* (Paris: Plon, 1972), p. 126.

16 As for twentieth-century manuals, one can cite editions up to 1968 of Armand Dunois, *Le Secrétaire universel* (1st edn, Paris: Garnier, 1858), or up to 1934 of *Le Secrétaire des familles* (1st edn, 1871).

Of the newcomers: Liselotte (pseudonym of Mademosielle Bouvard), *Le Guide de la correspondance* (Paris: Bibliothèque du 'Petit Echo de la Mode', 1925). Or, more recently, H. Fontenay, *La Bonne Correspondance: personnelle, commerciale et officielle* (Paris: Nathan, 1984), 284pp.

17 See Barbier, 'Une production multipliée'.

18 F. Barbier, 'Les Imprimeurs', in Chartier and Martin, *Histoire*, vol. 3, pp. 69–89.

19 Geographical distribution of signed and anonymous works:

	Signed	**Anonymous**	**Total**
Paris	80% (305)	56% (133)	438
North of the Loire	12% (49)	16% (37)	86
South of the Loire	8% (30)	28% (65)	95
Total	(384)	(235)	619

20 Cited by Darmon, *Le Colportage*, pp. 288–9.

21 See the essays by M. Melot, 'Le texte et l'image', and by S. Le Men, 'La vignette et la lettre', in Chartier and Martin, *Histoire*, vol. 3, pp. 287–311, 313–27.

22 Melot, 'Le texte et l'image', pp. 298–9.

23 One frontispiece, however, shows a man in the process of writing a letter, resting the paper on his knees. But the outer surroundings and the symbolic elements give the scene the seal of romanticism.

24 This dissymmetry is evident from the following table of statistics taken, by way of example, from the *Grand Secrétaire français*, published at least ten times between 1849 and 1883 by Le Bailly in Paris. It should be noted that male correspondence (two-thirds of the total) mainly concerns business, acts of allegiance and solidarity,

	ADDRESSEES			
	Men	**Women**	**Mixed**	**Total**
WRITERS				
Men	72	11	11	94
Women	7	1	5	13
Mixed	1	3	1	5
Total	80	15	17	112

but also family events (New Year's Day, births, marriages and deaths). The life cycle revolves around three figures: the schoolchild, the soldier and the head of the family and of the company. On the female side, there is a notable absence of young girls and a clustering of letter-writing on matters of marriage and wet-nurses.

25 One has to cite here the thesis written by C. Chotard-Lioret, 'La Sociabilité familiale en province: une correspondance privée entre 1870 and 1920', Ph.D. thesis, University of Paris-V, 1983; *Le Journal intime de Caroline B.*, enquiry by M. Perrot and G. Ribeill (Paris: Arthaud-Montalba, 1985). Also Geneviève Breton, *Journal*, 1867–1871 (Paris: Ramsay, 1985); *Marthe* (Paris: Éditions du Seuil, 1982) and *Émilie* (Paris: Éditions du Seuil, 1985). However, analysis that M.-C. Grassi has undertaken, based on a corpus of 1,100 letters written by members of the nobility between 1700 and 1860, provides a corrective to the idea that women played a pre-eminent role in letter-writing. According to Grassi's investigation, letter exchanges balanced out thus: 48 per cent of letters were sent by one man to another man; 15.5 per cent were from a man to a woman; 11 per cent from a woman to another woman; 25.5 per cent from a woman to a man. See Grassi's Ph.D. thesis, 'Correspondances intimes (1700–1860). Étude littéraire, stylistique et historique', University of Nice, 1985.

26 Three illustrations of amorous situations were included in manuals that did not focus specifically on the writing of love letters. Conversely, five illustrations of people writing were included in *secrétaires* specifically intended for lovers.

27 This is an allusion to the famous painting by Correggio, *Mercury teaching Cupid in the presence of Venus*, National Gallery, London.

28 See A.-M. Bassy, 'Le livre mis en pièce(s). Pensées détachées sur le livre romantique', *Romantisme*, no. 43 (1984), pp. 19–27.

29 Louis Philipon de La Madelaine, *Manuel épistolaire à l'usage de la jeunesse ou Instructions générales et particulières sur les divers genres de correspondance, suivies d'exemples puisés dans nos meilleurs écrivains* (Paris: Capelle et Renaud, year XII-1804), in-duodecimo, 370pp. This is a republication of *Modèles de lettres sur différents sujets* which Louis Philipon de La Madelaine had published in 1761 in Lyons (he was then twenty-seven years old). This 'revival' was followed by at least nineteen further editions between 1816 and 1871.

30 See Chartier and Martin, *Histoire*, vol. 3, pp. 188–9, 489–90.

31 Victoire Tinayre strove to defend the education of the popular masses through her active participation in mutual help societies and in consumer cooperatives. Under the Commune, she was the inspector of girls' schools in the 12th *arrondissement*. After her arrest and exile, she pursued her revolutionary activity in Switzerland and later lived in Hungary, according to the *Dictionnaire biographique du mouvement ouvrier français*, ed. E. Egrot and J. Maitron, vol. 9: *1864–1871*.

32 A.-M. Thiesse, 'Le roman populaire', in Chartier and Martin, *Histoire*, vol. 3, pp. 468–9.

33 For example, Zulma Carraud, *Lettres de famille . . .* (Paris: Hachette, 1855), and Baron Staffe, *La Correspondance dans toutes les circonstances de la vie* (Paris: Léon Chailley, 1895).

34 This is true of the manual compiled by Mathilde Bourdon, *Lettres à une jeune fille* (Paris: H. Casterman, 1859).

35 Eugène Crépet, *Le Trésor épistolaire de la France . . .* (Paris: Hachette, 1865). He is doubtless alluding to Puget de La Serre (1600–1665).

36 The *Grande Encyclopédie du XIXe siècle* and the *Dictionnaire de pédagogie et d'instruction primaire* by Ferdinand Buisson both echo this assessment.

37 C. Guimard, *Traité du style épistolaire . . .* (Nantes: from the author, 1850).

38 Descottez, *Nouveau Manuel épistolaire . . .* (Paris: Rue du Paon, 1837).

39 Louis-Charles Dezobry, *Dictionnaire pratique et critique de l'art épistolaire français* (Paris: Delagrave, 1866).

40 Edouard Sommer, *Manuel de l'art épistolaire* (Paris: Hachette, 1849).

41 See B. Beugnot, 'De l'invention épistolaire: à la manière de soi', in Bossis and Porter, *L'Épistolarité*, pp. 27–8.

42 Robert, *Grand et Nouveau Secrétaire général*... (Paris: Ferry, 1852).

43 100 models: Léon Lambert, *Le Petit Secrétaire galant*... (Paris: Les Marchands de Nouveautés, 1865). 125 models: H. Ferté, *Enseignement des jeunes filles. L'Art d'écrire une lettre*... (Paris: Hachette, 1894). 150 models: Léon Lambert, *Le Galant Secrétaire*... (Paris: Les Marchands de nouveautés, 1865). 200 models; V.-N. Duménil, *Le Secrétaire universel*... (Paris: Rue des Filles-St-Thomas, 1837). 340 models: P. Neckers, *Trois Cent Quarante manières de commencer et de finir une lettre*... (Renaix: Imprimerie Courtin, 1899). 1,000 models: Louis-Charles Dezobry, *Dictionnaire pratique et critique de l'art épistolaire français* (Paris: Delagrave, 1866).

44 Victor Doublet, *Cours pratique de compositions épistolaires*... (Paris: Delalain, 1850).

45 E.-G. Deiglun, *Exercices épistolaires*... (Marseilles, 1829).

46 Alexandre Abrant, *Exercices sur le style épistolaire*... (Paris: Larousse et Boyer, 1860).

47 L.-M. Roussenq, *Nouveau Recueil de lettres descriptives*... (Brignoles, 1837).

48 Abbot A.-J. Delbos, *Cours de style épistolaire*... (Paris: Lethielleux, 1860).

49 François Prudhomme, *Le Secrétaire général*... (Paris: Delarue, 1838).

50 Louis Delanoue (pseud. of François-Lubin Passard), *Manuel du secrétaire français*... (Paris: from the author, 1854).

51 A. Rossignon, *Exercices pratiques de style épistolaire*... (Paris: Belin, 1867).

52 The illustrations combine to confirm this elitist representation of letter-writing.

53 G.-C. Lhermitte, *Nouveau Manuel épistolaire*... (Paris: Camuzeaux, 1836).

54 Mlle Bochet, *Le Livre du jour de l'an et des fêtes* (Paris: Garnier, 1862).

55 H. Bescherelle, *L'Art de la correspondance*... (Paris: Dentu, 1858).

56 Narcisse-Honoré Cellier-Dufayel, *Cours historique et dramatique de style épistolaire*... (Paris: Chaix, 1847). George Sand, *Indiana* (Paris: Roret, 1837).

57 When Flaubert attempted to calm Louise Colet's jealousy, he did not hesitate to pour scorn on Eulalie Foucaud de Langlade, his 'passion' in Marseilles in 1840, on the grounds of her deplorable

spelling: she had written 'ottomate' instead of 'automate' (automaton). This howler unleashed Flaubert's mirth and, in his view, discredited its author (Gustave Flaubert, *Oeuvres complètes*, vol. 12: *Oeuvres diverses-Correspondance* (Paris: Club de l'Honnête Homme, 1974), p. 543, letter of 28 Sept. 1846). Flaubert was no doubt forgetting his own difficulties with spelling.

58 Henriette Large, *Traité de style épistolaire* . . . (Lyons: Vitte, 1894).

59 In anticipation of a critical study of representations and discourses on the 'natural' predisposition of women for letter-writing, one can usefully refer to F. Nies, 'Un genre féminin?', *Revue d'Histoire Littéraire de la France* (1978), pp. 994–1005.

60 *Format*: Octodecimo (known as Charpentier format, the most usual for novels from 1838 onward) dominates, above all in anonymous publications, followed closely by duodecimo. Sextodecimo is less frequent (one book in seven, approximately). Octavo, rarely used for anonymous works, is also used for signed works. Conversely, 32mo, generally uncommon, tended to be reserved for anonymous works.

Print run: It is materially impossible to locate letter-writing manuals in the mass of printers' statements in the F^{18} series in the Archives Nationales. The incompleteness of many titles, the absence of authors' names and the references only to publisher and year of publication make it impossible to identify works with any certainty. The odd clues that one can gather here and there amidst this store of statements testify to relatively large print runs: 2,000 to 3,000 copies. This means that letter-writing manuals were not far from novels in importance in nineteenth-century publishing. Although far below the print runs for 'classics' and school books, they surpassed the often modest runs of the great works of the century.

Pricing: Putting to one side those manuals produced abroad, which cost from 5 to 11 francs, and various large books (Dezobry, 1866, 15F; Alphonse Fresse-Montval, *Nouveau Manuel complet et gradué de l'art épistolaire* . . . (Paris: Poilleux, 1838), 7F; or Cellier-Dufayel, 1847, 5F), prices ranged from 1F to 3F. Works costing less than 1F (20c, 50c, 75c) were rare and did not appear until the turn of the century. Letter-writing manuals were averagely priced for the times, though with considerable variation depending on the quality of production. From what one can know of working-class budgets (established by Le Play, for example – see Frédéric Le Play (ed.), *Les Ouvriers des deux mondes*, 13 vols (1875–1912)), the cost of manuals placed them beyond the reach of most people, but within the reach of the middle classes.

Distribution: I have found a few titles of manuals among the lists of school books (Archives Nationales F^{17} 11651 to 11657) of the 1880s: the authors most valued by the inspectors were Zulma Carraud, Rossignon and d'Altemont – see Louis d'Altemont, *Narrations et lettres*... (Paris: Hachette, 1865).

61 *Guide pratique du style épistolaire*... (Paris: Laplace, Sanchez, 1873).

62 Adolphe Pécatier, *Parfait Secrétaire des amants*... (Paris: Veuve Desbleds, 1852).

63 A. Weill, *Lettres d'amour entre deux époux avant et après le mariage, depuis 1847 jusqu'à 1878* (Sauvaître, 1892).

64 Comtesse de Bradi, *Le Secrétaire du 19e siècle*... (Strasbourg: Veuve Berger-Levrault, 1840).

Index